There's a cry in the night that must be satisfied.

Every mother has heard it.

It's a cry that pierces sleep and raises weary heads

from pillows of comfort.

It's a cry that screams need and begs a mother's help.

This cry sounds from the soul of every child.

It is a cry of hunger for God.

Faith Feedings satisfies the cry in the night.

Published by
Deep River Books
Sisters, Oregon
www.deepriverbooks.com

ISBN: 9781940269528
Library of Congress: 2015939331

Printed in the USA

Design by Robin Black, InspirioDesign
Author image by Lime Green Room Photography

July 2015

Lisa —

May the LORD richly
bless your home and
family with a legacy
of faith.

Dee Dee Cass

Jeremiah 31:3

FAITH
feedings

Praise for *Faith Feedings*

At a time in church history when so many are laboring toward, praying for, and seeking after a revival, *Faith Feedings* may hold the key. Revival, if it is to truly come to God's people, will come, not within the walls of a church, but rather from under the rooftops of our homes. It will find its spark within the family dynamic, and it will be stoked as mothers (and fathers) pour the wisdom of divine truth into their children.

DeeDee Cass knows this; it is the heartbeat of her latest book. *Faith Feedings* takes square aim at capturing the hearts and minds of the church's youth by presenting mothers with a clearly articulated and inspiring call to nurture their children in the fear and admonition of the Lord. Taken directly from illustrative accounts in the biblical narrative, this invaluable resource walks readers through the crucial principles upon which godly parenting must be based. It equips them to navigate the challenges that are bound to come.

Written with the experience and insight of a mother, a grandmother, and someone who has devoted her life to ministry, *Faith Feedings* should be required reading for all mothers and mothers-to-be. It is essential, really, for anyone who hopes to mentor a son, a daughter, a grandchild, a niece, a nephew, or any other young person in her sphere of influence. This book will be a blessing to any family.

—MICHAEL G. SCALES, EdD, president,
Nyack College and Alliance Theological Seminary

As a pastor of children and youth, I am constantly looking for ways to encourage parents to be the leaders in the spiritual growth of their children. Parents not only *should* be invested in their children's spiritual walk, but *need* to be involved. Sadly, many mothers and fathers don't know how to do this.

As I read *Faith Feedings*, I was quickly convinced that it was of God. DeeDee Cass, one of the most Spirit-led women I know, has masterfully taken examples and truths from Scripture and organized them into an easily understood guide that is a must-read for any parent who desires to see their children grow in the Lord. Every mother—and father—in my church needs a copy.

—KEVIN GIANNOTTI, pastor of children and youth ministries, Bethlehem Church, Thornton PA

FAITH
feedings

12 PRINCIPLES TO
NOURISH YOUR
CHILD'S SPIRITUAL
DEVELOPMENT

DEEDEE CASS

Deep River
BOOKS

Dedicated to our next faith generation—my grandchildren,
Cooper, Adalene, Levi, Charles, and Oliver.

...let justice roll on like a river,
righteousness like a never-failing stream!
AMOS 5:24

CONTENTS

Foreword by Colleen Fraser 13

Preface 15

Introduction 19

The Charge 23

How *Faith Feedings* Works 25

PART I *Spiritual Milk* 27

    Faith Feeding 1   Ideal Mother 29

    Faith Feeding 2   Boy Jesus 39

    Faith Feeding 3   You Are God's Good Idea 49

    Faith Feeding 4   My Mother, My Grandmother 59

PART II *Living Water* 77

    Faith Feeding 5   Bad News Boys 79

    Faith Feeding 6   Cliff Climbing 89

    Faith Feeding 7   Hadassah's Story—God's Glory 99

    Faith Feeding 8   Nick's Night Job 109

PART III *Bread of Life* 123

    Faith Feeding 9   Boy to Man 125

    Faith Feeding 10   Exiled Faith 137

    Faith Feeding 11   For Goodness' Sake .147

    Faith Feeding 12   Wherever You Go .157

Epilogue The Return to Ramah Story 179

FOREWORD

I happen to be celebrating forty years with Cru (Campus Crusade for Christ) in the campus ministry this summer. I have had the privilege of impeccable training and biblical teaching over these many years, which I treasure. But the last eighteen years have made an exceptional impact on me. I attribute much of that to serving alongside DeeDee Cass in Community Bible Study.

It is one thing to hear great teaching; it is far more impactful to journey through life and ministry with a "living Bible." DeeDee would be the first one to say she is far from perfect and constantly dependent on God's grace with much to learn from the Bible. But at every turn and with every challenge I have observed DeeDee apply words of Scripture, often those she's memorized and, thus, coming from her heart.

I tell you this because what you are about to read comes straight from the heart and life of this dear and humble servant of God. The wise and practical words on these pages do not come from theories but from the direct application of the Word of God to her personal relationship with Christ and her family life. You will enjoy her insightful illustrations from her own life and family, as I have over the years.

DeeDee profoundly impacted me in the area of grace. "Grace, Colleen, grace." She must have said that to me hundreds of times. Where I was truth and accountability, DeeDee was the epitome of grace and patience. Over the years, God has used us in each other's lives, for which I am eternally grateful! I have learned much from both Paul and DeeDee Cass as I've watched them live out the Word of God through the power and grace of Jesus Christ.

That is why I am privileged to recommend this book. The practical principles in this book come from someone who has staked her life on them, living them out and pouring them into others, resulting in life changes.

In this book, DeeDee expresses the privilege that we have as mothers to model and teach our children about the Lord and his ways. I especially love the section about finding your child's unique "bent" and then cooperating with God to help them flourish in the special creation that they are. This is what I most wish I had known in my early years of mothering. I try to apply that now, but how wonderful it would have been to be building up my very young sons with focused intentionality. This book will be a great asset for every mother who desires to encourage and build up their children in godly character and their unique and precious design. I encourage teachers as well as all those who work in some way with children to read and apply these valuable lessons.

In Faith Feeding 6, DeeDee writes concerning 1 Samuel 14:7 where David's armor-bearer says, "Do all that you have in mind . . . Go ahead; I am with you heart and soul." She writes: "There is nothing that gives more encouragement than someone else to share your mission." That certainly defines our relationship from the first time I met DeeDee.

And so I say, "Go ahead, DeeDee. Do all that you have in mind. I am with you heart and soul."

My prayer for God's work through this book is:

Holy Father, may You use this book to revive the hearts of mothers toward You and toward their children. May You use it, O Lord, to raise up a generation of fully devoted Christ followers who impact the nation and the world with the character and grace of Jesus Christ shining through them, a beacon of light calling people out of the darkness into the kingdom of the Son You love (Col. 1:13-14). Amen (let it be established).

COLLEEN FRASER
Prayer Coordinator for Cru Mid-Atlantic Region

PREFACE

The search is over. The most influential person in the world has been found. She is close at hand. Her name is Mother. Make no mistake about it. If you are a mother, you are in a role of influence over your child. Your place of influence carries two greats: great privilege and great responsibility. This book, *Faith Feedings*, helps you provide a framework of godly influence around your child. It is a personal collection of verses and biblical principles that nourish faith in the next generation. I have used these Bible truths to integrate Scripture into the lives of my children and those young ones whom God has placed in my own circle of influence. Through this study of wisdom from the Bible, we will discover how to speak God's Word into our offspring as they grow into adulthood and beyond. The spiritual mandate of motherhood is to secure the conscience of your child for God. It is my calling and privilege to partner with you in this eternal and glorious mission.

This book is titled *Faith Feedings* because it embraces every child's need for faith nourishment. Nutrition is vital for life itself. Even in the womb God makes provision for sustenance and growth. Providing nourishment is the first responsibility of every mother, whether by bottle or by breast. Personally, I never fully grasped the magnitude of this responsibility until I decided to breast-feed our second child. I share this experience with you because breast-feeding so closely parallels the imparting of the spiritual development and nourishment principles I present in *Faith Feedings*.

My son was born back in the day, before lactation specialists and breast-feeding coaches. As a matter of fact, this newborn came with no feeding instructions. A night nurse in the hospital nursery came into my room and announced to me that it was time to feed my son. That was it. She plopped the little guy in my arms, and off she went. To be honest, my greatest concern was not his hunger. At the end of the day of delivery, all I could picture was falling asleep and dropping him out of the high hospital bed. It would be a hard one to explain to my husband, for sure. "Don't worry," said the nurse when she returned. "It will take a few days for your milk to come in."

Oh, the naivety of this 1970s mother. *Come in from where?* I thought, but pride kept me from asking. Well, the best I could tell, nothing "came in" before I took the little guy home. Once we were home, the whole family knew when I was trying to feed my son. All night long I tried to get a drop of nourishment into his tiny mouth. By the time morning came and my mother remarked that he "had a different look about him," I called the doctor. "I am not a neurotic breast-feeding mother," I exclaimed. (I lied!) "I am a doctor's wife who is starving her newborn." The pediatrician himself fed the babe his first bottle. *Bind her up. Breast-feeding is over for this one!*

You can imagine the shock expressed on my face when I took my son back for his six-week appointment and the doctor on call looked at me and said, "I hope you didn't try to breast-feed this baby. He has a congenital condition that makes feeding difficult. He'll outgrow it." Mark this newborn well-visit a success. The babe was healthy, and his mother was exonerated. *Can't wait to tell his father!*

Not to worry about my own breast-feeding experience. I have learned a thing or two about nature's milk supply thanks to my girls—the mothers of my grandchildren. For example, it matters what a mother eats. Caffeine and alcohol are restricted on a mom's menu for obvious reasons. Good nutrition benefits both mother and child. What I have learned relates to "faith feeding" as well. Just as what you eat affects your child, your child's faith is directly impacted by your own faith experience. Also, it is an established fact that the early relationship between mother and child is strengthened through feeding, whether by breast or

bottle. As you pass scriptural principles to your child, you will be foster-
ing a relationship that has eternal significance.

So break out your Boppy and the burp cloths. Your milk has come in.
There is a cry in the night that must be satisfied.

. . . you took in the sacred Scriptures with your mother's milk!
2 TIMOTHY 3:15 MSG

INTRODUCTION

I believe it is in the heart of every mother to do what is right and best for her children. But what is right and best is sometimes skewed. Education and opportunity have replaced meaning and purpose. Today's culture of entertainment and technology precludes biblical truths. What is important to our nation is transmitted via airwaves. Have you noticed what has sprung up on the hills and mountains across America? Communication towers. We are communicating the wrong message to our young people. Proverbs 18:10 says, "The name of the Lord is a strong tower. The righteous run to it and are safe."

Do not be fooled into thinking that this book is just for mothers of young families. Faith building is not limited to natural motherhood. If you are a mother, a grandmother, an aunt, a mother-in-law, a friend, or a neighbor you have the power to influence the next generation for Jesus Christ. You also have the responsibility.

My own grandmother opened the Scriptures for me as she helped me prepare to recite verses in vacation Bible school programs. From the day I was born, my aunt and uncle prayed for me to know the God of the Bible. My husband's mother lived the scriptural model of a mother-in-law. My friend invited me to my first Bible study. Each of these people supplemented the efforts of my mother and father to build a heritage of faith in their firstborn. My neighbors met with me regularly to validate the principles of this book as we learned together to press them into the hearts of the children on my street. My sister gave me the final impetus for the writing of this book. She strongly encouraged me to commit my thoughts to writing without further delay.

Passion for the Bible was stirred early in my life. As an elementary school student, I was asked to read Psalm 23 at an end-of-year event in my elementary school. On the surface, it was just a way to participate. I have often wondered if I was asked to read Scripture because I couldn't sing or was too tall to fit in with the dancers. In any case, once again, my grand-mother helped me prepare. On the day of the program, I stood before my peers and a parent audience. I vividly recall my own surprise as I spoke the psalmist's words from my heart without a glance at the white Bible in my hands. There are three things that are significant as I think about this memory. The first thing that comes to mind, regrettably, is that I would not be allowed to read the Bible in a public school setting today. Secondly, my grandmother's physical and spiritual presence and involvement in my life was crucial to my faith. The most touching thing, however, is simply that I was *asked* to read the Bible. The asking affirmed my faith. The real-ization that all those years ago my heavenly Father had begun to unravel his plan for my life confirms God's faithfulness and sovereignty.

The Bible is digested into our spirits "precept upon precept and line upon line" (Isa. 28:10 KJV). So it has been for me. In my early teens I mem-orized the King James Version of Matthew 5:16: "Let your light so shine before men that they may see your good works and glorify your Father which is in heaven." God has used this verse as a guide in my life. I can see now that this Bible passage was especially valuable in my youth. Then, as now, there were many pitfalls in the paths of the young. I am grateful for the pits I avoided because I had hidden these words in my heart and mind. Psalm 119:11 says, "I have hidden your word in my heart that I might not sin against you."

I relate all of this to you to communicate the early inspiration to faith in God that I received from the Word of God. Without it, I may have missed the greatest faith-growth opportunity of my life—an in-depth study of God's Word over a long period of time. In 1985, I began studying the Bible under the banner of Community Bible Study (CBS). There are many dif-ferent studies that offer excellent formal study of the Scriptures. However,

CBS is the one that God brought into my life and the one that I embraced. It is the one through which I have learned the purpose of the Bible. It is the one through which I have heard the call of God on my life. The riches of a daily and cumulative study of God's Word in any format takes one to a place of certainty and confidence in the Word that is best spoken by the prayer of Epaphras, a servant of Christ Jesus . . . "that you may stand firm in all the will of God, mature and fully assured" (Col. 4:12). Standing firm in all the will of God does not happen outside of the Word of God.

STANDING FIRM IN ALL THE WILL OF GOD
DOES NOT HAPPEN OUTSIDE OF THE WORD OF GOD.

It is in this confidence and assurance that I commit *Faith Feedings* to print. I do so trusting that the Lord will use his living Word in your life, mother, and the lives of your children. I do so in expectation that through our shared humble efforts, our great God will bring restoration faith to our families and a return in our land to the one true God.

As a servant of Christ Jesus, my prayer for you is that you use *Faith Feedings* as a model of providing spiritual nutrition for your children and family. I believe the truth of God's Word to the prophet Isaiah: "So it is with the word that goes out from my mouth: It will not return to me empty, but will accomplish what I desire and achieve the purpose for which I sent it" (Isa. 55:11). Therefore, I pray that the Word will accomplish its work in your life and in the life of your child. I pray that you will come to know the love of God and the God of love through the integration of these biblical precepts into your family. I pray that you and your offspring "may stand firm in all the will of God, mature and fully assured" (Col. 4:12). "May the Lord direct your hearts into God's love and Christ's perseverance" (2 Thess. 3:5). And I pray this prayer in the One whose Name is a strong tower, Jesus Christ.

It is obvious that we cannot rely on education, culture, technology, or government to build a heritage of faith in the next generation. This eternal task is ours to do. Let's make it a picnic. B.Y.O.B.—Bring Your Own Bible, of course, and get ready to spread out your godly influence. Your child has been fashioned with a hunger for God; begin speaking God into their lives today.

My soul will be satisfied as with the richest of foods.

Psalm 63:5

THE CHARGE
The Lord Is My Shepherd

The unofficial results are in. Psalm 23 is the most requested reading at Christian memorial services and funerals. And it is rightly so. David's treatise on his Lord, the Shepherd, exudes comfort to the grief-stricken. It pictures those who have departed in green pastures, beside still waters, and with a restored soul. You already know that David's words about the Shepherd and the sheep are meaningful to me, so allow me to make an official request: I would like Psalm 23 read at my farewell service. Now let me share something with you. The Word of God is for the living. Let me speak the first three verses over you now. Read aloud with me:

> *The Lord is my shepherd; I shall not be in want.*
> *He makes me to lie down in green pastures;*
> *He leads me beside the still waters.*
> *He restores my soul;*
> *He leads me in the paths of righteousness for his name's sake.*

David's background was shepherding; he knew sheep. David also knew the human heart and soul. His early life, after he was anointed king of Israel, was anything but regal. He was a shepherd on the run. King Saul's jealousy caused him to scorn David, and he spent years in the desert far away from the green pastures and quiet waters he loved so much. David was also a singer and composer. His beautiful poems reveal his dependence on God. David knew God as the shepherd's Shepherd. David's Shepherd was the Provider of all he needed.

Nothing suits a sheep's appetite more than green pastures. Nothing calms a sheep's nervous stomach like quiet waters. Nothing is more important to a sheep than its relationship with its shepherd. A restored soul is a must. And where would sheep go if their present pasture were depleted? No worry there. The shepherd would choose the path and guide them in it. The shepherd always knows the right path.

The shepherd on the mountainside and the Shepherd in the heavens take personal responsibility for their flocks. They both care for their sheep physically, emotionally, and spiritually. The question for us as mothers is this: If the shepherd cares for the whole sheep, how can we do less for the little ones of our flock? One question always leads to another: Doesn't most of the time with our children go into meeting their physical needs? Our homes are in supply-and-demand mode. We supply food to relieve hunger, transportation to activities, and help with homework, not to mention hugs and BAND-AIDs for hurts. Society says that is enough, but if we were truthful with each other, we would confess that in our hearts we know better. Enough is only enough if it includes the eternal dimension of your child's soul. But where in the world will you find the time to elevate your child's spiritual condition to the same level as their physical and emotional needs? We have now arrived at the essence of *Faith Feedings*.

I am not asking you to add God to your already packed life. Rather, it is my deepest desire that you unpack your life and discover God in it. He is already there. He has been there all along. He is your Shepherd who supplies everything you need. He is your green pasture and your quiet water. Yes, may He guide us in paths of righteousness for his Name's sake and for the sake of his Name in the next generation.

Know that the Lord is God. It is he who made us, and we are his;
We are his people; the sheep of his pasture.
PSALM 100:3

HOW *FAITH FEEDINGS* WORKS

*F*aith Feedings is a personal collection of biblical principles that serves to build and nurture faith in the next generation. The aim of *Faith Feedings* is to equip readers with a unique and inspirational method of integrating Scripture into the lives of their children. Seeking to maximize faith influence within the family, *Faith Feedings* is designed to leverage a child's conscience toward God and a mother's desire to do what is right for her offspring.

Faith Feedings is divided into three main parts: Spiritual Milk, Living Water, and Bread of Life. These section titles represent the progression of nutrition from milk to solid food. They also denote the process of spiritual maturity in the life of a person of faith. The book is further divided into twelve *Faith Feedings*. Each *Faith Feeding* has four elements:

1. **The Story.** Each story relates a biblical account as an example of the application of Scripture to personal circumstances. The Word of God demonstrates the power of God at work in the frailty of human beings. The Story allows readers to identify with Bible characters and encourages them to trust God with their own imperfections.

2. **The Nourishment.** Each nourishment principle is a specific verse from the Bible that serves to impart faith. The goal of this book is to nurture faith by the integration and use of Scripture. The Nourishment element of *Faith Feedings*

teaches readers how to apply the precepts of the Bible to their own life and the lives of their family members.

3. **The Lesson.** Each lesson illustrates the *Faith Feeding* principle by examining the context of the Bible passage of The Story and Bible verse that is presented as a godly life principle. The lessons give background information as it relates to Old and New Testament times and the present. The Lesson segments of each *Faith Feeding* feature topics that help the reader use the unique approach of *Faith Feeding* as nutrition for the faith of the next generation.

4. **The Point to Faith.** Each faith point recaps The Nourishment element and encourages the reader to act. Every *Faith Feeding* ends with a prayer that encourages the inclusion of God in the faith heritage–building process.

PART I

Spiritual Milk

You must crave pure spiritual milk
so that you can grow into
the fullness of your salvation.
Cry out for this nourishment
as a baby cries for milk,
now that you have had a taste
of the Lord's kindness.

1 PETER 2:2-3 NLT

*Meanwhile, the boy Samuel grew up
in the presence of the Lord.*

1 SAMUEL 2:21

IDEAL MOTHER

THE STORY

(SEE 1 SAMUEL 1:1-2:26)

L ife for Hannah was anything but ideal. In the early Jewish culture, a wife without children was scorned—especially one without a son. Descendants were the promise of the covenant with Father Abraham. No offspring? No part in the promise. If Hannah had lived on my street back in the day, the sight from her window would have brought her to bitter tears. The question, "Why has the Lord closed my womb?" would have played through her mind like a familiar song. The mothers congregating and the children playing would have fueled her thoughts of failure and lack of purpose. Sad to say we would have agreed with Hannah's assessment of herself. Unfortunately, our society still scrutinizes the childless couple.

Hannah had a wonderful husband, Elkanah, who loved God and his wife. He often told her how much he loved her, but it seems he didn't really understand her childless plight. He also did not understand the daily trauma she faced. Hannah had company in her marriage to Elkanah; her name was Peninnah. There were two differences between Hannah and Elkanah's other wife. Peninnah had children, while Hannah had none.

And Elkanah loved Hannah more than Peninnah. Can you imagine the strife in that camp?

It was Elkanah's longtime custom to travel with the family to Shiloh for an annual sacrifice. On one such occasion, Peninnah provoked Hannah so much that she took desperate measures: "In bitterness of soul Hannah wept much and prayed to the Lord" (1 Sam. 1:10).

Hannah's prayer was so fervent that Eli, the priest, mistook her utterances for drunkenness. Hannah made a vow to the Lord that if she were given a son she would "give him to the Lord for all the days of his life" (1 Sam. 1:11). In time, the Lord answered Hannah's prayer. She named her son Samuel, which sounds like the Hebrew word for "heard of God." After Samuel was weaned from his mother's milk, Hannah kept her promise. She took Samuel to Eli in Shiloh and left him there to grow in the Lord's service.

Can you imagine Hannah's days and nights of anguish over her son? *Is he safe? Is he being fed properly? What will he be like when I see him again?* Such thoughts about her son prompted Hannah to make a special gift. "Samuel was ministering before the Lord—a boy wearing a linen ephod. Each year his mother made him a little robe and took it to him when she went up with her husband to offer the annual sacrifice" (1 Sam. 2:18-19).

Ponder that robe. As women, we know it gave Hannah hope. She probably wasn't through the city gate before she began planning next year's robe. Such thoughts would have taken away the sting of parting from Samuel year after year. The biggest question Hannah had to answer each year was the size of the next robe. She had to evaluate her son's present stature and estimate a year's growth. Hannah knew the robe she was making was not an ordinary garment. She understood the spiritual significance of a linen ephod. God himself had fashioned the priestly robes, and it was for God himself that Samuel was being raised to serve. The annual robe was a statement of faith that Samuel had, indeed, been a gift from God. The robe changed as Hannah's faith grew. No doubt with every stitch there was a prayer that young Samuel would grow to be a man of godly character and purpose. Hannah's handiwork framed Samuel's physical, spiritual, and emotional growth in his early childhood. The yearly Growing Robes were markers of Hannah's hopes and dreams for her son.

So what made Hannah an ideal mother? Certainly, her days before Samuel was born were not ideal. In addition, there was nothing ideal about a mother who only saw her young son once a year. But Hannah lived out daily her faith and trust in the Lord, and that would have been evident to Samuel. And can you imagine her joy at knowing God had answered her prayer? And most significantly, no doubt, were her ongoing prayers for her son. The Scriptures reveal that Hannah had an ideal attitude. "I prayed for this child, and the Lord has granted me what I asked of him. So now I give him to the Lord. For his whole life he will be given over to the Lord" (1 Sam. 1:27-28). God was gracious to Hannah, the mother of godly ideals. After Samuel, she birthed three sons and two daughters. Hannah truly was a woman of the promise.

THE NOURISHMENT

Meanwhile, the boy Samuel grew up in the presence of the Lord.
1 SAMUEL 2:21

Modern mothers have a tremendous advantage over Hannah. We live in the day of God's grace. We can raise our children in the presence of the Lord in our own homes. We do not have to leave them behind in Shiloh and practice absentee motherhood. If God is in our heart, He is in our homes. If God is in our heart, He is in our cars. If God is in our heart, He is in the grocery store, the doctor's office, and at the beach.

IF GOD IS IN OUR HEART, HE IS IN THE GROCERY STORE, THE DOCTOR'S OFFICE, AND AT THE BEACH.

Meanwhile, wherever you are with your child, take the lead from Hannah. When your child tickles your heart, bring God into the moment. Say to your daughter or son, "I am so glad God made me your mother," or "What a gift from God you are to me," or even "You are an answer to prayer." Every time you connect your child with God, you raise their level of awareness of God's supernatural presence in their life.

Motherhood is lived in "the meanwhiles," the commonplace spaces between events. Look for opportunities to express your gratitude to God for their presence in your life. Doing so will affirm God's faithfulness in your own life and integrate God's faithfulness in your child's life. In the meanwhile, you will be teaching your child to grow up in the presence of the Lord. It sounds ideal to me!

Blessed are those who have learned to acclaim you,
Who walk in the light of your presence, O Lord.
PSALM 89:15

THE LESSON

The author of both of the books of Samuel was not sparing in his words about Samuel's parents, Elkanah and Hannah. Samuel was groomed to do great things for God. The lessons of his upbringing are important to us as we groom our own children for the same.

We can surely identify with Hannah as a young mother who committed her son to service to the Lord. In emotional terms, it was probably the hardest thing she ever did. In her heart, however, she knew she had done what was right in God's eyes. Hannah expressed her spiritual confidence in a prayer recorded in 1 Samuel 2:1-10. Hannah's prayer, written in poetry form, is a song of joy and peace emanating from a heart of gratitude for her firstborn. I recall such sentiment in my own heart after the birth of my firstborn. All those years ago, long before I knew Hannah, I chose a birth announcement with these words: "A gift from God who brings joy to our hearts and peace to our souls." Indeed, if you are a mother, you have sung the same song. You may not have written it or even spoken it. You may not have acknowledged God or even believed in God at the time. The circumstances of your life may not have warranted a song of gratitude. That was then. This is now. Search your heart. Find your song and sing it. Thank God for his hand in your child's life. Hannah knew the joy of the gift of her child and so do you. Inviting God into the realm of your motherhood is the first taste of nutrition for the faith of your child.

Samuel's father, Elkanah, teaches us an important faith lesson as well. "Year after year this man went up from his town to worship and sacrifice to the Lord Almighty" (1 Sam. 1:3). Elkanah consistently practiced his faith in his family. You can be sure that between visits to Shiloh he lived a godly life before his wives and children. It also pleases me to know how Elkanah supported Hannah's decision to entrust Samuel to Eli. "Then Elkanah went home to Ramah, but the boy ministered before the Lord under Eli the priest" (1 Sam. 2:11).

My husband, who honors my faith in God, has enriched my life. The value I place on a husband's faith support is illustrated in a conversation I had many years ago with my children. It was in the early fall, just after the beginning of a new school year. The smell of cookies in the oven set the stage for one of those golden moments. A dear friend had been killed in a car accident during the previous summer. My deceased friend's son and my daughter were the same age, and she expressed her concern for him.

"I am sad that he is coming home from school to no mother."

I agreed and assured her that even though his mother was not with him now, he had good memories of their conversations. I knew that my friend had often shared with her son the things she valued. Suddenly, from around my table, one of my children blurted out the question of a lifetime.

"What would you want us to know if you were not here?"

I remember the thoughts that flew through my mind. There were many good answers to that question. I could tell them to be faithful to the Lord, to make good moral decisions, to bring glory to God in all they do. And then I spoke to my daughter and son. "The one thing I love most about your father is that he shares my faith. Find a husband or wife who will share your faith as well."

Praise God, they did just that! It is amazing to me that neither my son nor my daughter remembers this specific after-school discussion. But it does not amaze me that God remembers it.

If we are honest, we will confess that it would have been better had Elkanah not taken a second wife. The Bible doesn't tell us whether he just gave in to the pressure of his culture to produce a descendant. Perhaps he thought it would remove pressure from his barren wife. Either way, God used it as a rub in Hannah's life that deepened her dependence on the Lord. Is there a rub in your life now that God is using for a greater purpose? Perhaps there is a circumstance or a relationship that is wearing you down. Follow Hannah's example. Pour your heart out to God and do what you know to be right. When you reflect on this season of your life, you will see that the trial you are experiencing is God filtered. God does not waste "rubs." Rather, he uses them to draw you to Himself. Think of Hannah and be encouraged to trust the Lord in all things.

As a couple in the Lord, Elkanah and Hannah carried out their lives in faith. But it is the lesson that we learn from Hannah's yearly sewing project that speaks to our Faith Feeding theme. "Samuel was ministering before the Lord—a boy wearing a linen ephod. Each year his mother made him a little robe and took it to him when she went up with her husband to offer the annual sacrifice" (1 Sam. 2:18-19). Before Hannah cut the linen cloth or made the first stitch, she had to estimate Samuel's likely growth. The robe had to be a garment into which Samuel could grow. I call it a Growing Robe, and the concept of Hannah's Growing Robe is the key to faith nurturing. Let's work through these steps together to maximize our faith parenting.

1. Sketch a robe or make a robe cutout from paper for each of your children. Accurately evaluate them according to gifts/tendencies; strengths/weaknesses; what they enjoy doing/what needs to be more prevalent in their lives. As you make your list, look beyond normal child development to character and faith development. List your observations on the "robe."

2. Pray that God will help you to see your child through his eyes and that He will help you make them an appropriate robe. Most of all, ask the Lord to give you the wisdom as a mother to help them develop according to their Growing Robe.

3. Know that this robe is a garment of faith in God. Your personal faith is the thread. As your faith in God deepens and changes, the robe will change. Your heavenly Father has made for you a Growing Robe. Where are you now in your relationship with God? What do you think God wants you to look like in a year? What steps can you take to fit into your God-made robe? God's mirror is the Bible. His scale is woman friendly. His love is without strings. His grace is sufficient. His hope is endless.

My young neighbor provides a great example of something to list on our Growing Robes. Several months ago, my mother was transported by ambulance from our home to the hospital. When I returned home later that day, I found a handmade card in our mailbox. In a rainbow of marker colors it read, "Dear Nana, I hope you get well!! We are praying for you in our hearts. We all love you so much! We are praying to GOD to keep you *helthey* [sic]! God bless you." This precious child believes that God answers prayers. What a great concept of faith to affirm! Write it on her Growing Robe then find ways to grow that character in her. Ask her to say the blessing at meals. Pray with her at bedtime. Give her a small notebook to record her prayers in short phrases. Most importantly, let her hear you pray and tell her when God answers your prayers.

Another example was provided by a toddler who sat next to his large dog. The child let loose with a rather long and loud passing of gas. Immediately, the child looked at me and said, "It was the dog." I was astounded at his early awareness that the sound of gas needed to be blamed on someone else. His understanding of the concept of telling a fib shocked me. Alas! Innocence broken at such an early age! But fabrication is normal for children. They are so unaware of their transparency. If your child has a penchant, however, for speaking untruths, write it on his Robe. Then remind him or her (or them) that it pleases God most when we tell the truth. Be sure you, too, are a model of truthfulness for your little ones.

I am sure you are beginning to understand the pattern of the Growing Robe. The Bible verses and principles that we will feast on in the next eleven chapters will provide faith-growing opportunities for you and yours. As you watch your child grow into the Growing Robe you have fashioned, you will discover Hannah's secret. Motherhood's greatest privilege is also motherhood's greatest responsibility—fashioning Growing Robes for the children God has granted us.

Have you noticed? I have sewn a robe for you. It is a one-of-a-kind designer ephod made of fine linen. Your robe is flattering to your God-shape and becoming to your unique gifts and graces. Your faith garment reveals your beauty—even in God's three-way mirror. I exhort you to put it on. It's a keeper. Go ahead, mother, pass it on to the next generation. It's yours to give.

Back to Hannah. Every year, she and Elkanah returned to their home in Ramah after visiting their son. It would be eleven months before she would see Samuel again. Every day she would pray and every day she would plan for the next visit, but on no day would she be provoked or irritated by Peninnah. She would just sing her song: "My heart rejoices in the Lord" (1 Sam. 2:1). It would surely be music to Elkanah's ears.

I thank my God every time I remember you.
In all my prayers for all of you,
I always pray with joy . . . being confident of this,
that he who began a good work in you will carry it
on to completion until the day of Christ Jesus.
PHILIPPIANS 1:3-4, 6

THE POINT TO FAITH

Meanwhile, the boy grew up in the presence of the Lord.
1 SAMUEL 2:21

Have you ever pictured yourself as one who could bring the presence of the Lord to your child? What an awesome thought! Ask God to radiate his presence through you and look for opportunities to express your faith. Let your child hear you give God the glory and thanksgiving for his or her existence.

PRAYER: *Heavenly Father, thank You for being present in my life. I pray that You will bless me with the wisdom and understanding needed to grow faith in my child. Bring others across their paths that will strengthen them in their relationship with You. In Jesus' Name I pray. Amen.*

And Jesus grew in wisdom and in stature
and in favor with God and men.

LUKE 2:52

BOY JESUS

THE STORY

(SEE LUKE 2:21-52)

Have you heard of families who unknowingly left children at rest stops? You think one child is with another family member and off you go. Without a headcount, you could be way down the road before you discover the missing sibling. All of a sudden, after shrieks of "Where's Johnny?" panic sets in. It is striking that this very thing happened to Joseph and Mary centuries ago. On their yearly trek to Jerusalem for the Feast of the Passover, they traveled with literally everyone from their town. After the Feast, they would join up to travel home. The story about their sixty-five–mile trip is told in Luke 2:41-52. After a whole day's travel, they were shocked to find that their boy, Jesus, was not among the caravan.

"Have you seen Jesus?" was the Hebrew cry. Immediately, Mary and Joseph hurried back to Jerusalem. You can imagine the questions they asked each other along the way: *Where will we look for him? Has he been harmed? Is he frightened? What is he eating?* Jerusalem was a well-populated city, even after the pilgrims went home. We can identify with the sense of panic that overtook them as they searched for Jesus. But not to worry; He was exactly where you would think He would be. That is, if you knew that He was the Son of God. Jesus was in the temple sitting with the teachers. Luke 2:47 tells us that "everyone who heard him was amazed at his understanding and answers."

This story of boy Jesus is fascinating since we know so little about his life as a child. One thing we do know is that Mary, his mother, had to grow into the knowledge of the true identity of her son. The angel Gabriel had informed her about the Son she would bear, but the future of Jesus was a mystery to her. Even though Simeon, a devout and righteous man from Jerusalem, and Anna, the prophetess, had confirmed that Jesus was the Christ, Mary wondered about her son. Luke 2:19 says, "Mary treasured up all these things and pondered them in her heart." In a small way, mothers can really appreciate Mary's heart as she watched Jesus grow. We, too, see gifts and graces in our own children and wonder what the future holds for them. Signs of wisdom and maturity give us deep pleasure. We also treasure in our hearts our children's journey.

This story ends well. "Jesus went down to Nazareth with them and was obedient to them" (Luke 2:51). Amen to that! The very last commentary on Jesus from this passage is found in verse 52, "And Jesus grew in wisdom and stature, and in favor with God and men."

This growth chart evaluation of Jesus is aptly placed after his meaningful experience in the temple and the record of his obedience to his parents. No doubt Mary pondered a certain hopeful future for her boy. The unnerving experience of a lost son was over, and she breathed a sigh of thanksgiving for his protection and gratitude for his obedience. In every mile to their home, I think Mary was washed with a sense of awe and blessing about what she had observed in her son at the temple.

The Nourishment

And Jesus grew in wisdom and in stature,
and favor with God and men.

Luke 2:52

These very same words were used to describe young Samuel. "And the boy Samuel continued to grow in stature and in favor with the Lord and with men" (1 Sam. 2:26). Whether directed toward Jesus or Samuel or your very own child, such words are a yardstick of godly growth. This scriptural accolade encompasses physical development, godly wisdom, and right relationship with God and their peers.

There are times when you observe an accomplishment or maturity in your child, and it gives you a feeling of satisfaction to see them growing in a specific area of their life. That is the time for you to affirm your child with this verse from Luke. The speaking of these words will be a time of highest praise for them.

LOOK FOR A MARKER IN YOUR CHILD'S PROGRESS AND CHARACTER. PLACE YOUR HAND ON THEIR SHOULDER AND REPEAT LUKE 2:52 USING THEIR NAME.

Look for a marker in your child's progress and character. Place your hand on their shoulder and repeat Luke 2:52 using their name. "And (*your child's name*) grew in wisdom and in stature and in favor with God and men." Over time, this affirmation will genuinely bless your child with the knowledge that they are on the right path. It will positively reinforce wisdom and maturity in them. These words will verify what is good in them and give them a desire to continue in the same direction.

Jesus' early childhood is likewise described in Luke 2:40. "And the child grew and became strong; he was filled with wisdom, and the grace of God was on him." Use these words as a prayer for your young one. Speaking God's language to your child and speaking to God about your child will unleash a powerful dynamic in their life.

All Scripture is God-breathed and is useful for teaching, rebuking, correcting and training in righteousness.
2 Timothy 3:16

The Lesson

Luke was a detail man and wrote his Gospel to underscore the humanity of Jesus. As a physician, he had a perspective of human life that shines through in his words. It is especially meaningful to mothers that he gave an account of Jesus' mother, Mary. From Luke we have insight on the "carpenter family" that helps us with our own.

Mary is honored in Scripture and rightly so. After all, she is the link to Jesus' humanity. The Son of God, given for the sake of humanity, found his humanity in Mary's womb. It was Mary's high calling to bring this Child into the world. In every unfolding aspect of her son's life, she witnessed the unfolding of God's Son. Jesus' birth in Bethlehem and his death on a cross outside of Jerusalem were like bookends in Mary's heart. Everything in between fulfilled the words spoken to her by the angel Gabriel. "Do not be afraid, Mary, you have found favor with God. You will be with child and give birth to a son, and you are to give him the name Jesus. He will be great and will be called the Son of God the Most High" (Luke 1:30-32).

There is not a mother among us who does not realize that her child is not Divine (or divine for that matter). However, each one of us shares

Mary's hope that our child will live a purposeful life according to God's plan. An angel didn't announce our son or daughter, but we do have God's Word to speak to us about God's perspective of our child. "For you created me in my inmost being; you knit me together in my mother's womb . . . My frame was not hidden from you when I was made in the secret place . . . your eyes saw my unformed body. All the days ordained for me were written in your book before one of them came to be" (Ps. 139:13, 15-16). These words indicate that God is uniquely involved in the personhood of our children. Nobody understood that principle better than Mary. Every detail of Jesus' life revealed God's presence and power. Every glimpse of God in her boy caused her to live out Luke 2:19: "Mary treasured up all these things and pondered them in her heart."

Luke records two early instances in Jesus' life that affirmed what Mary knew in her heart. Like Elkanah and Hannah, Joseph and Mary lived according to the custom of the Law of Moses. They knew the words of Exodus 13:2: "Consecrate to me every firstborn male." So they took Jesus to Jerusalem to present him to the Lord. While they were there, they met two very important people in the earthly life of Jesus. The first was Simeon. Luke 2:25 says that Simeon was "righteous and devout . . . and the Holy Spirit was upon him." Simeon had been waiting his whole life to see the Messiah. God had promised him "he would not die before he saw the Lord's Christ" (Luke 2:26). God's Spirit led Simeon through the temple courts on the day that Jesus was brought to Jerusalem for his consecration. When he found Joseph and Mary's child, Simeon took him in his arms and identified the babe as the long-awaited Savior. Can you imagine what was going through Mary's mind? An angel had told the shepherds in the field about Jesus' birth. Now she had to consider Simeon's words. She knew the origin of her infant, the shepherds knew it (Luke 2:8-20), and now this godly man of Jerusalem, whom she had never seen before, knew it as well. It is no wonder the Scripture says in Luke 2:33, "The child's father and mother marveled at what was said about him."

As if that were not enough, the "carpenter family" also met Anna, the prophetess, in the temple. I love that God sent a woman to Mary that day. The Jews had great respect for the elderly and for widows. Anna's thanksgiving to God for the life of Jesus, who would be the redemption of Israel, would have deeply blessed Mary's mother's heart. My guess is that Mary hung on Anna's words for years to come.

Have you ever had anyone confirm a glimpse of God in you? Even more important, have you ever confirmed a glimpse of God in someone else? Do not tarry to do so. It is your calling as a woman of faith. It is one of those things that may be left forever unspoken if it does not come from your lips. Glimpses of God are everyday occurrences. Pray that God will bring them to your attention, then purpose to identify godly traits and growth in others and actively respond to them.

Such an opportunity presented itself to me recently. Michelle (not her real name) is the middle child of a family that joined our church several years ago. I have watched her grow from a cute little girl to a lovely young woman. From the time she was old enough she has worked at a local Italian restaurant. I am a frequent take-out customer at that establishment and see Michelle often (more often than I care to admit). On my recent pickup of an Italian hoagie and a Philly cheesesteak, I was met by her beautiful smile. Our conversation centered on her high school graduation.

"What an exciting time for you," I said. "This is the freest time of your life. Enjoy every minute of it. Tell me about your plans for next year."

Michelle went on to share with me the name of the university she would be attending and the course of study she would take. With take-out in hand, I said to this college-bound sweetheart, "I see that you are a godly young woman and are grounded in your faith. You will have the wisdom to make wise decisions. Surround yourself with like-minded friends. I am excited for the path you have chosen. God bless you, Michelle."

A two-minute take-out pickup gave me an opportunity to speak a blessing on her life. Prayerfully, God will use my words to encourage

Michelle's young faith. She will need it when her feet hit the campus. Have you ever thought of yourself as one who could actually confirm a glimpse of God in another? Just think of the eternal benefit you could impart to those God has brought into your circle of influence. It is no accident that my church friend is also my take-out friend. Be intentional about confirming glimpses of God in others and anticipate God doing a mighty work in their lives. It will become the joy of your living. My prayer is that someone will come along and confirm the glimpse of God in you. I see God in you. Why else were you led to read this book? Take it and run with it, mother. It is my joy to anticipate the mighty work God is about to do in your life.

In Jesus' lifetime, Mary would see many glimpses of God. He would amaze the Jewish leaders with his insight into the Scriptures; He would bring healing and deliverance through miracles; He would live his life with compassion for the poor and humble. At every turn, this mother recognized God's hand on her son. At the wedding in Cana, she would prompt Jesus to turn the water into wine. She knew. She had always known. As the angel told her before she conceived Jesus, "For nothing is impossible with God" (Luke 1:37). The beautiful thing about Mary is that she believed God with all her heart. It was her belief that prompted her to say, "I am the Lord's servant . . . May it be to me as you have said" (Luke 1:38).

Our Faith Feeding verse for this principle encourages us to look for glimpses of God in our children and affirm them by saying, "And (*child's name*) grew in wisdom and stature and in favor with God and men." Keep in mind that we are not looking for success or social graces. We are looking for evidence of God's character in their lives. When we find it, we use the verse to let them know in a consistent way that they have responded to life in a wise and biblical way. I recall a time when my young daughter showed forgiveness to someone who had hurt her. *And Kelly grew . . .* On one specific occasion my son showed godly compassion for his friend whose parents had recently divorced. *And Jeremy grew . . .* My children are grown now, and they are parents themselves. Nevertheless, I am still looking for glimpses of God in them. They will never be too old to be affirmed by Luke 2:52.

I realize that you may be a mother with a special-needs child. Perhaps your child is not able to grow in wisdom and stature. Perhaps favor is not in their scope. That does not mean, however, that you will not see glimpses of God in them. You will see his power and presence in their lives in ways that will make you marvel. This concept is beautifully illustrated in the life of Meg Olivia.

Meg was one of those extraordinary children who had a powerful influence on others in spite of her disability and short life span. Meg was born with anencephaly (congenital absence of all or part of the brain). In every one of her 917 days on earth, this babe without a developed brain revealed glimpses of God. Her parents fully integrated her into their family life. What an influence she had on the children around her! She shaped their life sensitivity. Meg's mother has shared with me that through Meg she saw God's sovereign hand. This mother had the peace of knowing that God had numbered Meg Olivia's days in weeks and months when she was unsure if there would be another twenty-four hours for her daughter. If Meg could have spoken to her mother, she would have said, "And my mommy grew in wisdom and stature and in favor with God and men."

With every day of her child's life, Mary trusted God's sovereignty as well. After all, Simeon had told her "a sword would pierce her own soul too" (Luke 2:35). At the foot of the cross, as Mary watched her son suffer and die for the sins of the world, did she really believe it was over? I do not think so. And she was not disappointed, for Luke tells us in Acts 1 that two men dressed in white said to the assembled disciples, "Why do you stand here looking into the sky? This same Jesus, who has been taken from you into heaven, will come back in the same way you have seen him go into heaven" (Acts 1:10-11). And so we wait with Mary for a glimpse of Jesus in the sky.

*When Joseph and Mary had done everything required by
the Law of the Lord, they returned to Galilee to their own town of
Nazareth. And the child grew and became strong; he was filled
with wisdom, and the grace of God was upon him.*
LUKE 2:39-40

THE POINT TO FAITH

---

*And Jesus grew in wisdom and stature
and in favor with God and man.*
LUKE 2:52

Did your child do something today that demonstrated godly character? Be intentional about speaking Luke 2:52 using their name. It will send a message about what is important to you and to God. As you commend your child in this way, your faith will grow as well. Every time it is spoken, Luke 2:52 will remind you of God's faithfulness to you as a parent.

PRAYER: *Dear Jesus, allow me to see and affirm godliness in my child. Help me to use this verse to encourage those in my care in the way they should walk as your children. Bless You for the model You are for the next generation and me. In Jesus' Name I pray. Amen.*

FAITH FEEDING 3

Then God said, "Let us make man in our own image, in our likeness." ... So God created man in his own image, in the image of God he created him; male and female he created them.

GENESIS 1:26-27

YOU ARE GOD'S GOOD IDEA

THE STORY

(SEE GENESIS 1)

Have you had any good ideas lately? History is filled with accounts of people who brought their good ideas to reality. Take a young medical student in 1932. After observing heart surgeries, he made a wheel-like device. Years later, Michael DeBakey's good idea would be revealed to the world as part of an artificial heart. We all know how the brilliance of men and women over time has improved on Dr. DeBakey's good idea. The human heart transplant has replaced the artificial heart implant. Perhaps one of your loved ones lives and breathes with the heart of another. Thank God for man's good ideas that help others.

God's good ideas are different from those that humans express. They are not a starting place. They do not leave room for improvement. God's good ideas are perfect and complete at their inception and implementation.

Thousands of years after the creation of the world, God spoke through the prophet Isaiah about his Word. He said, "My word that goes out from my mouth . . . will accomplish what I desire and achieve the purpose for which it I sent it" (Isa. 55:11). This verse is perfectly illustrated in the creation account. Listen, then, to God's Word:

- *And God said, "Let there be light," and there was light . . .*
  God saw that the light was good.

  GENESIS 1:3

- *And God said, "Let there be an expanse between the waters*
  to separate water from water." . . . And it was so . . . God
  called the expanse "sky" . . . And God said, "Let the water
  under the sky be gathered into one place, and let dry ground
  appear." . . . And it was so . . . God called the dry ground
  "land" and the gathered waters he called "seas." And God
  saw that it was good.

  GENESIS 1:6-10

- *Then God said, "Let the land produce vegetation: seed*
  bearing plants and trees on the land that bear fruit with
  seed in it according to their kinds." And it was so. And God
  saw that it was good.

  GENESIS 1:11-12

- *And God said, "Let there be lights in the expanse of the sky*
  to separate the day from the night, and let them serve as
  signs to mark seasons and days and years and let them be
  lights in the expanse of the sky to give light on earth." And
  it was so. And God saw that it was good.

  GENESIS 1:14-15, 18

- *And God said, "Let the water teem with living creatures,*
  and let the birds fly above the earth across the expanse of
  the sky." . . . And God saw that it was good.

  GENESIS 1:20-21

• *And God said, "Let the land produce living creatures according to their kinds." And it was so . . . And God saw that it was good.*

GENESIS 1:24-25

God said, "Let . . ." and it was so . . . and God saw that it was good. After God spoke his good idea into existence by the power of his Word, He critiqued his handiwork. And God said it was good. In Genesis 1:31, God evaluates His creation work: "God saw all that he had made and it was very good."

But wait a minute! Something is missing. We have light and land and skies and seas. There are plants and creatures of the air and of the earth. But God had another good idea. "Then God said, 'Let us make man in our own image, in our likeness.' . . . So God created man in his own image, in the image of God he created them; male and female he created them" (Gen. 1:26-27). You are God's good idea! And before He brought you into reality, He prepared a place for you that would sustain you and offer you vitality, meaning, and purpose; a place where He could meet with you; a place where God the Creator could be with man and woman; a place of blessing and fellowship and timeless provision. *You* are the crowning glory of all God's creation. *You* are God's good idea!

The Nourishment

Then God said, "Let us make man in our own image, in our likeness." . . . So God created man in his own image, in the image of God he created him; male and female he created them.

GENESIS 1:26-27

You are God's good idea and so is your child. Speak often to your children about how God values them. Give them "God-esteem."

Replace their self-image with God-image. This understanding serves as a shield against unkind words, failure, and poor self-image. It will produce in them confidence, purpose, value of others, and reliance on their Creator. Knowing this truth from the Bible will give them a strong sense of their own identity and a desire to remain true to it. Emphasize the truth that what God thinks about them outweighs what the world describes as good. God says they are good, very good. God loves what He created.

AS YOU CONNECT YOUR CHILDREN'S INDIVIDUALITY
WITH GOD'S POWER TO CREATE,
YOU WILL RAISE THEIR SENSE OF SECURITY.

Overlay this concept onto your children by affirming the God-given tendencies and characteristics you see in them. *God made you so* (kind, funny, loving, honest . . .). *God gave you* (a grateful heart, a good mind, great talent . . .). *God loves your* (cheerful heart, gentle spirit, obedience . . .). As you connect your children's individuality with God's power to create, you will raise their sense of security.

The God who created them has a personal stake in their lives. They are not alone. They are loved regardless of their lack. They have significance that overshadows the opinions of others. What an advantage in life they will have knowing "in his image he created them!"

The creation account is crucial to faith in God. To dismiss God from the beginning is to dismiss God from the ending and everything in between. Make "In the beginning God" the foundation of your child's faith.

By faith we understand that the universe was made at God's command,
So that what was seen was not made out of what was visible.
HEBREWS 11:3

THE LESSON

Picture this scene in a hospital in central Pennsylvania in the early 1950s. A young mother peered through the glass at her newborn daughter. Her heart was filled with joy over the child for whom she had waited. Her tender thoughts were interrupted by the voice of another onlooker. "Do you see that baby girl? She has only one hand. I hear the mother is just going crazy."

The mother replied, "I am that baby's mother, and I am just fine."

While this scene unfolded in the hospital, I was in my grandmother's kitchen, sitting on my favorite shiny red, upholstered chair. Sometimes I would sit on that chair holding a block of oleo. I would work it in my hands until it became spreadable. On that day, however, I had a different experience. My life changed. My grandmother told me that God had given me a special sister; she was born with only her left hand. With my seven-year-old heart I believed her. My sister was special.

My mother remembers the face of that other mother; I remember the chair. And a lifetime confirms that my sister is surely God's good idea. Not long ago I asked my mother, now 92 years old, to tell me again about the conversation at the nursery window. She was quick to repeat the story. This time, however, she added something new. When she addressed the lady at the nursery window she was expressing for the first time her acceptance of her special little girl. She truly believed her daughter was a beautiful gift from God. At that moment, our mother demonstrated her faith in Genesis 1:1 "In the beginning God . . . " These four words change everything.

"In the beginning God" changes the way we view the sunrise and the sunset, what we see in the night sky. Those four words change what we hear singing in a tree or crying in a cradle.

"In the beginning God . . . " determines our perspective of our own selves, of others, even of our enemies. Because of those words, our relationships are different. They change how we view our husbands, our wives, our children, our friends, our neighbors. Therefore, they impact our marriages, our families, our communities, our nation, and the world.

Looking back, I realize that handicaps were viewed differently in the 1950s and '60s. There was no advocacy or access as we have now. I have often considered my parents wise beyond themselves regarding how they raised my sister. They saw her as a child with two hands, and they pushed the "you can do it" envelope. A university doctor commended my parents when my sister was only two for the balanced strength in both of her arms. It makes me laugh that as my sister grew, her mantra could have been "anything you can do, I can do better." Though I was seven years older, her "can do" showed up my "can do" on a regular basis. That makes me grateful for our mother and father's wisdom toward me as well.

Having the faith to believe Genesis 1 is crucial to godly parenting. If you do not have it, ask God to give you such faith. If you have even a grain of Genesis 1 faith, ask God to give you the wisdom and the way to pass it on to your children. Belief in God as your Creator is vital to peace and fulfillment in your life. From it flows a sense of value and comprehension of personal identity. In turn, assurance of value and identity shape influence. Value, identity, and influence are three "must" characteristics for the Growing Robes we are fashioning for our children.

VALUE

What value does something that came from nothing have except that it came from God? When God created the heavens and the earth, He did not begin with already present substances. Rather, He created all things. The God who made something from nothing is the God who made you. You are God's intent. When "I am God's intent" shouts louder than "I am worthless," life takes on eternal meaning and purpose.

In our homes and schools, our young people are revealing a value crisis. "I am valuable" is being drowned out by the "I am too's"—too tall, too fat, too ugly, too thin, too anything but God's good idea. Every day we hear value indices: the strength of the dollar, the price of gold, the rise and fall of stocks. And every day we hear the results of the value famine of the human soul: insecurity, moral failure, addiction, eating disorders, bullying, crime, murder, suicide. "Then God said, let us make man in our own image, in our likeness" (Gen. 1:26). Now there's a value index. Those fourteen words are like rain from heaven. They replace self-image with God-image. Together let's bring on the rain and end the self-worth famine in our own lives and in the lives of those we influence. We live in an age of labels and logos; "Made By God" surpasses them all.

IDENTITY

Personal identity goes beyond name and family lines. Our children want to be what they are not. What they want to be is determined by what they find appealing in others. My young daughter, who is musically talented, once asked me why God hadn't made her a cheerleader. She's an amazing musician but wanted to be something else, something more popular. Our tendency to want to be anything other than what we are is fed by our lack of the understanding of our identity. Everywhere we turn in our culture we are encouraged to forsake ourselves and become what is popular or successful. The only way out of this lie is to know our true identity. True identity is not found in our earthly heritage. True identity originates with our heavenly Father. When we know the truth of whose we are, we will have the freedom to choose who we will become. The pathway of our life will reveal decisions based on confidence, security, and innate assurance. Now, mothers, isn't that what we want for those who have been entrusted to our care?

Our story, Boy Jesus, illustrates this identity principle. In Luke 2:49, Jesus says to his parents, "Why were you searching for me? Didn't you know I had to be in my Father's house?" Because Jesus knew his own identity, He knew He was doing what He was meant to do. Such assurance of purpose, undoubtedly, is a missing element in today's child. We have a great opportunity to edify our children by helping them realize their value to God and grasp their identity in Him. What a privilege! What a responsibility!

INFLUENCE

If there is one thing this generation is missing, it is awareness of the individual's power to influence others. Influence is forever linked with value and identity. Children who know their value to God and their identity in God will find meaning and purpose in being an influence for God. As the oldest grandchild in the family, I recall the numerous times my mother reminded me of the influence I had on my sister and cousins. As I grew, I became aware of a wider circle of influence. Knowing the possibility of my influence on others shaped many of my personal choices as a young person. Every child needs to grasp their potential for influence because every child needs to know that their life matters.

Value, identity, and influence are three pillars of your child's faith growth. With these pillars in place, he or she will know the following:

- a heavenly Creator who designed them
- a heavenly Father who loves them
- a heavenly purpose to fulfill them

When my mother looked in the nursery window that day, she saw a beautiful baby to care for and love. When God looked at the baby girl, He saw his good idea. I have had the privilege to see God's plan unfold in my sister's life. As a mother and aunt, my sister is a delight to the children in our families. I have always marveled at her relationship with my daughter and son. They will long remember their aunt's words of encouragement when they have a challenging task: "You are loved, and you are capable." Those words ring true in a person who knows she is God's good idea. They are apt words for you as well. "You are loved, and you are capable." Do not be sparing in making certain that your children know the same.

The Lord does not look at the things man looks at. Man looks at the
outward appearance, but the Lord looks at the heart.
1 SAMUEL 16:7

THE POINT TO FAITH

Then God said, "Let us make man in our own image,
in our likeness." . . . So God created man in his own image,
in the image of God he created them;
male and female he created them.
GENESIS 1:26-27

All children deserve to know their value to God. Can you imagine
how different life would be for our young people if they truly believed
they were God created? Also, how different would the world be if they
knew the same about others? A child is never too young to hear you
whisper in their ear, "You are special to God."

PRAYER: *Lord God, thank You for creating me as I am. Help my*
family to understand in a deeper way how much You value each one of us.
May we, in turn, value each other and the ones You bring into our lives. In
Jesus' Name I pray. Amen.

FAITH FEEDING 4

Train up a child in the way he should go,
and when he is old he will not turn from it.

PROVERBS 22-6

MY MOTHER, MY GRANDMOTHER

THE STORY

(SEE 1 AND 2 TIMOTHY)

Timothy was the name given to the pride and joy of Mother Eunice and Grandmother Lois. Dad was proud, too, but as a Greek, he left the training in Judaism to the women of the household. And train Timothy they did. As a young child Timothy understood the value of faith in Yahweh, the one true God. He knew and abided by the Law of Moses. When he was a young man, he met a man who became like a father to him. That man was the apostle Paul. Paul became Timothy's spiritual father when Timothy heard and believed Paul's preaching about Jesus. Timothy demonstrated that he was a man of strength and principle when he was circumcised as an adult so that he would have credibility with Jews and Gentiles alike. Over and over in his letters to the early churches, Paul calls Timothy a son, a brother, and a fellow worker in spreading the gospel. We learn from Paul's letters that Timothy was a courageous leader in spite of his timid spirit and sensitivity.

Paul spent three years in Ephesus developing faith in Christ in the church there. Paul thought so much of Timothy that he left him in Ephesus to continue his work. Timothy is to be admired as a pastor of the church in Ephesus. Ephesus was a worldly city filled with idol worship and hostility to Christians. Timothy was young to take responsibility for the church at Ephesus. He did not disappoint, however. By his example, he taught Christians how to live and prove their faith in God through Jesus.

Paul spoke highly about Timothy in his letter to the Philippian church. He wrote, "I have no one else like [Timothy], who takes genuine interest in your welfare. For everyone looks out for his own interests, not those of Jesus Christ. But you know that Timothy has proved himself, because as a son with his father he has served with me in the work of the gospel" (Phil. 2:20-22).

What more could we want for our children than to have them be a Timothy in their own generation? Reared in faith and responsible as a member of the church and community, Timothy used his gifts and graces to encourage the faith of others. He was accomplished in his work and compassionate in his relationships. In Paul's second letter to Timothy, he encouraged him: "To Timothy my dear son . . . I thank God whom I serve . . . as night and day I constantly remember you in my prayers. Recalling your tears, I long to see you so that I may be filled with joy. I have been reminded of your sincere faith, which first lived in your grandmother Lois and in your mother Eunice and, I am persuaded now lives in you" (2 Tim. 1:2-5). These affirming words from his mentor, Paul, would have strengthened Timothy in his role as a servant of the Lord.

Would we not all want our children to be so valued and fulfilled in their life's work as was Timothy? Would we not want them to have healthy and secure relationships? Timothy was trained up according to his way and he never departed from it. Well done, Lois and Eunice!

You then, my son, be strong in the grace that is Christ Jesus.
2 TIMOTHY 2:1

THE NOURISHMENT

*Train up a child in the way he should go, and when he is old
he will not turn from it.*

PROVERBS 22:6

This verse pictures a child who is set apart by his parent's instruction to demonstrate morals and living out their faith. Proverbs 22:6 exhorts us as parents to train a child according to Christian principles and tradition, and when he is grown, he will continue in them. Clearly, early faith nourishment contributes to the adult walk of our children. This fact should encourage us to be diligent about speaking God into our young offspring and teaching them early about their faith. There is, however, another aspect of this verse that has given me deeper understanding of my role as a parent. According to the Greek-Hebrew dictionary, "in the way he should go" can be translated to mean in the manner he was designed or created. The Hebrew word *derek* is the key. Derek is the word used for *way* in the original translation. One of the meanings of this Hebrew word is manner. It corresponds to our English word *bent*. With this meaning, the verse would say, "Train up a child according to the way God intended him to be, and when he is old he will not depart from it."

While I fully endorse the original translation of Proverbs 22:6, I have found the second understanding to be a valuable parenting perspective. There is great merit in treating your child according to his bent. If, as mothers, we fully acknowledge the unique, godly design of our children, we help them become what God fashioned them to be and live a life of fulfillment. To that end, I encourage you to look for what puts a glint in your child's eye. Relate to your child by honoring and accepting the way he or she was created by God. Encourage each one according to his/her personality, skills, giftedness, and inclinations. Ask God for discernment and wisdom as you strive to develop characteristics in your child that will lead to fulfillment. Fulfilled children lack frustration and are well adjusted in adulthood. Here is my own proverb on the subject: A glint in the eye well nourished produces a lilt in the gait long cherished.

There are many practical building blocks to faith that will last a lifetime. Daily reading of a children's Bible will plant the stories of biblical characters with strengths and weaknesses just like their own. They will see how much others have needed God and the great things God has done in Bible history. Attending church as a family on a regular basis develops a practice that they will need as they face the many Sunday morning alternatives that present themselves as they age. One of the greatest aids to faith that your adult children will experience is recalling a familiar hymn or praise song from their childhood. It will give them a sense of the longstanding tenets of faith. In our day there are numerous sources of enriching music and Scripture songs that will find a home deep in their hearts. Faith-inspired music will play in their minds for a lifetime. Make music a part of their childhood faith experience from the crib to the family minivan.

TAKE ADVANTAGE OF THE INCREDIBLE ABILITY THAT THE YOUNG HAVE TO MEMORIZE AND RETAIN REPEATED WORDS AND PHRASES. MAKE THEIR HEARTS A STOREHOUSE OF GOD'S WORD.

There is one faith building block that will strengthen and encourage faith in youth and adults like no other—Scripture memorization. Psalm 119:11 flags the value of embedding God's Word in the hearts and minds of your children: "I have hidden your word in my heart that I may not sin against you." Take advantage of the incredible ability that the young have to memorize and retain repeated words and phrases. Make their hearts a storehouse of God's Word. Over a lifetime, God will be faithful to bring stored Bible verses to their minds as they make decisions and face challenges. They will be ever grateful for the treasures of the Bible that you have helped them deposit in the eternal vault of their hearts. Make accruing spiritual wealth through memorizing Scripture a priority discipline for you and those entrusted to your care.

In my book, *The Scripture Code . . . Unlocking Spiritual Wealth*, I introduce and detail a model of Bible memorization. This method uses the first letter of each word as a memory prompt. When I teach this method to children, I relate it to their own initials. They can envision how their initials stand for their name and then can apply it to a verse of Scripture. I have been thrilled with testimonies of children in Sunday school classes, Bible studies, and youth groups using *The Scripture Code* to internalize God's Word. Let me give you an example. Fear plagues all children. What if children had a verse to repeat when they became afraid? Psalm 118:6 says, "The Lord is with me; I will not be afraid." In *The Scripture Code*, that would be written like this: T L i w m; I w n b a-f. Psalm 118:6. Now put it into action.

Write these letters on a card and teach your young ones what these "initials" stand for in *The Scripture Code*. If you really want to have fun, grab your bucket of sidewalk chalk. If your street is like mine, this Scripture memory method will be like a magnet to draw other children who also need to be assured of the presence of God. Be prepared. Ministry is on your doorstep!

In addition to Bible reading, Scripture memorization, church attendance, and faith music, teach your children to pray. Thank God for the food at mealtimes, ask God for safety on trips, and share with God the daily concerns of your child. In this way, they will learn that God is one who hears them and cares for them. From childhood prayers they will learn to rely on God and to wait on God for the answers to their prayer. They will need that trust and patience as an adult. When the answers come—"yes," "no," or "not now"—be sure to praise God for his faithfulness.

From my own childhood, I learned a biblical principle from a seemingly simple statement. In the corner of my grandmother's living room was a table with a Bible on it. Once, I placed something on top of the Bible. With very gentle words my grandmother said, "We never place anything on top of the Bible." Without even being aware of it, my grandmother communicated to me the value she placed on God's Word. To this day, I hear her words when I am stacking my books. The Bible is always on top. More importantly, I have come to understand what she really meant all those years ago.

As I grow older in the Lord, I am becoming increasingly aware of the need to impart faith in Jesus Christ to the next generation. It is my grievous observation, however, that the conscience of the next generation toward God is waning. Children have a great propensity for belief in God. Perhaps that is the heart condition behind Jesus' words in Luke 18:17: "I tell you the truth, anyone who will not receive the kingdom of God like a little child will never enter it." Life is full of opportunities to prick a child's God conscience. Many of those opportunities come at times of special holidays like Christmas and Easter. Do you have special traditions in your family that help to create a faith memory for your children? If our family pictures are ever put in order, they will reveal the yearly reading of the Christmas story that takes place before the giving of gifts. It delights me to see my adult children and my grandchildren climb into our bed on Christmas mornings for the reading of Luke 2. It has become a reverent time to hear Dad or Grand Paulie read from the Bible about Mary and Joseph's journey to Bethlehem for the birth of their son.

Think about Christmas mornings in your home. Do you have a faith memory-maker in place? Some families sing Happy Birthday to Jesus. Others list the gifts God has given them before giving gifts to each other. Do not miss the window of opportunity that Christmas provides. Enlarge the conscience of your children toward God by celebrating the true meaning of Christmas. It is a faith reflection they will carry with them through all their lives.

Think, too, about the calendar holiday that is the crux of the Christian faith—Easter. Do you have a favorite Easter memory such as egg hunts or special treats from the Easter bunny? My kids would probably mention the time our dog, Casey, ate all the chocolate candy while we were at church. We were glad he was still alive on Easter Monday. Personally, I recall two things about the Easters of my childhood. One is that my mother saw to it that we received the largest chocolate rabbit on the planet and a new Easter outfit. The other is the one-mile walk down the hill with my grandmother to attend a three-hour Good Friday service at our home church. Two hymns play in my mind from those services— "The Old Rugged Cross" and "Were You There?" As I think back, I realize that my grandmother raised my consciousness of Jesus in our arm-in-arm walks to church for Good Friday and regular evening services.

Whether by formal teaching, faith memories, or the personal testimonies of your faith, allow Proverbs 22:6 to be a daily yardstick of faith training and godly development of your child as a unique and worthy individual. Fully embrace your spiritual responsibility as the matriarch of the family to secure for God the conscience of your next generation. Look forward to hearing God's accolade reserved just for you: "Well done, good and faithful servant!" (Matt. 25:21).

> *. . . fan into flame the gift that is in you . . .*
> *for God did not give us a spirit of timidity,*
> *but a spirit of power, of love and of self-discipline.*
> 2 TIMOTHY 1:5-7

THE LESSON

Timothy's name, which means honoring God, reflects the high hopes that Eunice and Lois had for their boy. But do you think for a moment that Lois and Eunice knew the influence they really had on him? They just did what they knew to be right according to the Scriptures, and God carried out his plan for his servant, Timothy. Many times Eunice might have been concerned that Timothy was so timid and sensitive. She must have been shocked when Timothy began to travel with the apostle Paul. Paul was known for his stringent adherence to the Truth of the Bible and high expectations. Yet, Paul and Timothy became as a father and son serving the Lord Jesus together. So close were they that Paul left Timothy in charge of the ministry he knew he would not complete. Paul was facing death for being a Christian, and he appointed his young protégé to continue his work.

As history would have it, Timothy was the one who actually received, in the form of a letter, the last written words of the greatest evangelist and church builder of all time, the apostle Paul. In his last letter, Paul wrote to Timothy: "I have been reminded of your sincere faith, which first lived in your grandmother Lois and in your mother Eunice and, I am persuaded, now lives in you also" (2 Tim. 1:5). These words are affirmation of the influence of a mother and a grandmother on the faith of their offspring. That, mothers, is the crowning glory of motherhood: that our faith would live on in our children.

In 1 Timothy 6:11-12 Paul charges Timothy to pursue righteousness, godliness, faith, love, endurance, and gentleness. To fight the good fight of the faith, and to take hold of the eternal life to which he was called. Paul discerned the fulfillment that Timothy received by exercising his God-given gifts and talents. He recognized Timothy's capacity for leadership and service in the kingdom of God. This validation of Timothy's true identity was a powerful force in the next generation from Lois and Eunice. It is pure joy when another sees the glint in our child's eye, like Paul understood Timothy.

Questions are begging to be asked here. Have you identified the glint in your child's eye? If so, have you accepted and validated it? I strongly advocate identifying and supporting the unique predispositions that each child has. I think of the young people on my street. One chases after space travel. Another is keen on bringing health and well-being to others. Yet another is pursuing his dream of flying military jets. None of these hopefuls arrived at their present understanding of their personal bent independent of nurturing and encouragement given by others.

George, a member of our faith community, was a great example of one who cared about the giftedness of young people. George invested himself in the futures of those he knew. He identified their strengths and exhorted each one to develop their skills. At his memorial service, he was commended for how he had inspired our children. It is risky business to commit to inspiring your son or daughter toward their personal bent. It may not be conventional to the family. It may be radically different than the glint in the eyes of your other children or even your own inclinations. Often it requires you to give up your own hopes and dreams for their hopes and dreams. And always it demands wisdom and prayer . . . lots and lots of prayer.

The first book of the Bible I studied was the book of James. It is a great book of practical ways to successfully live the Christian life. I recommend that you read James every year on your birthday. An offer from God concerning wisdom is presented early in James. "If any of you lacks wisdom, he should ask God, who gives generously to all, without finding fault, and it will be given to him. But when he asks he must believe and not doubt" (James 1:5-6). I asked. The wisdom I needed concerned my son, who was born with a strong glint for knowledge in his eye. From early on, he had intense interest in specific areas. He had a passion for teaching and amassing facts. At bedtime, my son preferred the world atlas to a compelling story. As a mother, I was challenged to know how to respond to his desire to explore and learn. One morning as I watched him go up the driveway to catch the school bus, I received my answer. Words flooded my mind and heart: *Let him be what he was meant to be.* I understood the message immediately. I must parent him according to his unique design, allowing him the freedom to grow into the "robe" that God had designed for him (see Faith Feeding 1). In hindsight, I am grateful for the wisdom that came to me while he was young. Surely I would have stifled his bent if left to my own way. When my son got off the bus that day, he had a new mom waiting for him. She was one that was committed to cooperating with God's gifting of His child.

Passage of time has given me the privilege of seeing the glint in the eyes of the next generation of our family. It does not surprise me that my son's daughter and sons have strong glints in their own eyes. Each of them reflects traits and interests of their mother and father. One loves to create stories and songs, and the other loves technology and how things work. Peace emanates from the youngest. A certain joy of grandparenting is watching glints unfold before your very eyes.

I am reminded of a father who shared with me his frustration with his teenage son. He said that his boy was enamored with building with Legos™. The father thought the son was too old to "play" with children's blocks and threatened to throw them in the trash. Perhaps the young man needed some boundaries and limits to his Lego passion, but denying his desire to build and create was unwise.

Rebellion lurks in those whose gifts and graces are stinted. What does your child love to do? What puts a sparkle in his eye? Are they creative and lean toward art or music? Are they caring and have a passion for animals and needy people? Are they curious and love to delve into science and discovery? Maybe they're athletic and graced with natural quickness and eye-hand coordination. Or perhaps they shine in the spiritual realm and are drawn to things of God. Are they prone to teach or write or perform or speak in front of others? Do not delay, Mom, to do two things: Employ James 1:5 (ask God for wisdom) and draw up a lesson plan for your child. Inspire them toward being what they were meant to be. And one more thing; don't forget the boundaries and limits. Every child needs to participate in the family, showing respect to the "glint in the eye" of others and responsibility for their actions.

Now it is time to address what I believe is the original intent of Proverbs 22:6: raising a child to know and love God in such a way that they embrace it all the days of their life. Surely, this was the goal of Timothy's mother and grandmother. Instilling within Timothy a faith in God was their daily passion. Passion for faith is contagious in our homes. As the person of influence in your child's life, you must model what you want to impart. If it is faith you want to impart, then you must bear the fruit of faith in your own life. I think Timothy would have seen three characteristics of faith in the women of his home: grace, contentment, and a servant's heart.

GRACE

Has someone ever given you something you know you did not deserve? Perhaps a gift or a privilege was bestowed on you that exceeded your merit. It is a beautiful thing to realize that what you have received exceeds your ability to procure it for yourself. So it is with God's grace. Not only does God give us the faith to believe, He gives us the grace to make our faith worthwhile. The ultimate gift of life is the unmerited favor that redeems us through God's Son, Jesus. Paul called Titus "my true son in our common faith" (Titus 1:4). In his letter to Titus, Paul wrote, "When the kindness and love of God our Savior appeared, he saved us, not because of the righteous things we had done, but because of his mercy" (Titus 3:4). And to the Ephesians Paul wrote, "For by grace we have been saved through faith— and this is not from yourselves, it is the gift of God" (Eph. 2:8). We who have received the grace of God are administrators of the grace of God (1 Pet. 4:10). Our "first recipients" are our children. We are as Eunice and Lois to them. So how should this grace look to our children? Consider these characteristics of biblical grace:

✝ is not mere kindness	✝ fuels forgiveness
✝ exceeds justice	✝ expresses righteousness
✝ overrides wrongs	✝ surpasses worldly wisdom
✝ exudes humility	✝ frames our identity

How should grace look to our children? It should look like unmerited favor bestowed by their mother on those who are undeserving. In principle, bestowing grace is regifting what you have been given. Practically, it is treating those you encounter, beginning with your family, in a way that is distinguishable from the world's treatment. Grace loves the unlovely. Grace pardons the offensive. Grace rewards the undeserving. Grace forgives the unforgivable. Grace extends mercy to the unmerciful and helps the helpless. Grace, in the words of a plaque given to me by a dear friend, is "going outside of yourself to find what is best in another."

The key to grace giving is that it comes only from the God of grace. We have no grace to give on our own but must rely on the grace that God has poured on us through the person of Jesus Christ. Deep grace giving requires deep grace receiving. Grace comes to us through a consistent daily relationship with the Lord that includes Bible reading, Scripture memorization, and prayer. This reality came to me through a saying I once heard: "One day out of the Bible and I know it. Two days out and my family knows it. Three days out and the whole world knows it." In his home, Timothy witnessed the riches of God's grace in his mother and grandmother. They lived and practiced the words of "Amazing Grace" as penned by John Newton, the nineteenth-century hymn writer. So, too, must we. Paul said it best in his exhortation to the believers in the early church: " . . . continue in the grace of God" (Acts 13:43). Make these six words of Bible wisdom your daily marching orders.

CONTENTMENT

Recently, a local church sign grabbed my attention. It said, "This Week's Sermon Title: All I Want Is More." Would that sign have caught your eye as well? Actually, I am surprised that my community was not breaking down the doors to hear that sermon. The idea of having more is the mantra of our society. It is the American dream. It inspires our actions and rules our hearts. But wanting more is not godly, unless, of course, the goal is to want more of God. Apostle Paul learned the lesson of contentment in his life. Philippians 4:11-13 reveals his thoughts on contentment: "For I have learned to be content whatever the circumstances. I know what it is to be in need, and I know what it is to have plenty. I have learned the secret in being content in any and every situation, whether well fed or hungry, whether in plenty or want. I can do everything through him who gives me strength."

Secret? There is a secret to contentment? Everyone wants to know a secret! If you want to have a lasting faith impact on your child, you want to know the secret of contentment, too. The secret is not in knowing the best investment strategies or the best bargains. The secret is in knowing the source of your strength. He who gives you strength is He who gives you grace. Paul himself reveals his source of strength in his prayer for the church at Ephesus. "I pray that out of his glorious riches he may strengthen you with power through his Holy Spirit in your inner being" (Eph. 3:16).

Contentment, then, comes from being satisfied with what you have because you know that your strength is in the Lord, not in more of what the world has to offer. Immediate action: Go to your garage and scrape "The One With the Most Toys Wins!" bumper sticker off your car. Replace it with your own version: "Content to Be Content." "I can do everything through him who gives me strength" (Phil. 4:13) highlights Paul's belief that his success is dependent on God's power in him, rather than the empowerment of having more. Personally, this verse means that if God can make me content, nothing I encounter in Christ will be impossible. Like grace, contentment requires a deep relationship with God, who is the source of your strength. And like grace, contentment must be developed in your life over time. Impart faith to your child by asking God to impart contentment to your soul through his Holy Spirit. Oh, to go back in time and see the words burned into the wooden cart that Lois and Eunice used to go to market! My guess is that they said, "Content to Be Content" . . . in Hebrew and Greek, of course.

A SERVANT'S HEART

"To serve or be served," that is the question. The answer comes from Jesus Himself in response to a mother's ambition for her sons who were Jesus' disciples. The mother of Zebedee's sons, James and John, asked a favor of Jesus. She requested that her two sons sit at the right and left of

Jesus in heaven. Her request provided a perfect backdrop for Jesus' teaching on greatness.

Matthew 20:26-28 says, "Not so with you. Instead, whoever wants to become great among you must be your servant, and whoever wants to be first must be your slave—just as the Son of man did not come to be served, but to serve, and to give his life for a ransom for many." I can picture James and John's mother wanting to disappear into the crowd after hearing Jesus' response to her. Her idea of greatness was just rejected by the King of Kings! Let's not be too hard on Mrs. Zebedee, however. We all want what is best for our children. Service has a secret just like contentment. Serving others is at the top of Jesus' "How to Be Great" list. On the night before Jesus' death, he modeled practical service to his disciples. He washed their dusty and, no doubt, crusty feet.

John 13:12-17 says:

> *When he had finished washing their feet, he put on his clothes and returned to his place. "Do you understand what I have done for you?" he asked them. "You call me 'Teacher' and 'Lord,' for that is what I am. Now that I, your Lord and Teacher, have washed your feet, you should wash one another's feet. I have set you an example that you should do as I have done to you. I tell you the truth, no servant is greater than his master, nor is a messenger greater than the one who sent him. Now that you know these things, you will be blessed if you do them."*

While we are not likely to walk around with a towel and a basin looking for feet to wash, we can follow Jesus' service model every day. Servanthood is in Jesus' DNA. So should it be in ours as mothers of faith. Serving others is not doing until we drop or serving without regard for our own well-being. Our service to others springs from the attitude of our hearts. It is living life as one who has received the ultimate service.

Jesus served humanity by becoming human. We serve humanity by becoming divine. Servanthood takes on the character of Christ, for the sake of Christ. It is never unnoticed by the One in whose Name we serve.

This point was pounded home to me one day when I was pairing and folding my husband's socks. I had a reputation in the family for losing socks in the washing machine. Trying to be helpful, my mother-in-law even bought me those little rings to keep sock pairs together in the washer. That only meant I now lost both socks and rings. Add to this my husband's penchant for taking one sock off inside out, and sock folding was a frustrating task. On this particular day, a verse came to mind that I had read in my Bible that very morning, Colossians 3:17: "And whatever you do, whether in word or deed, do it all in the name of the Lord." There it was, right before me. The socks were secondary. A heart to serve following the model of Jesus is what matters. I always had a natural inclination for service. Now it had a divine dimension to it. Colossians 3:17, in conjunction with Colossians 3:24, which reads, "It is the Lord Christ you are serving," applies to menial tasks and privileged service alike. There is nothing like the joy of Christlike service. "Now that you know these things you will be blessed if you do them" (John 13:17). Timothy grew to be a man who served the Lord and others in ways he never dreamed possible. He saw it first in his home.

This is a call to all mothers who have faith of any quantity. Employ Proverbs 22:6 every day of your children's life. Train them up according to the glint in their eye. Make their passion your passion. Train them up according to your model of faith. Make your passion their passion. Follow Jesus' example in a practical way. He didn't just tell his disciples about faith; he showed them faith in action. He extended grace to all. He was content with his lowly state as the Son of Man (see Philippians 2:6-11). He washed their feet and their souls by serving them in life and in death. Let your children see your faith in action—in your gracious acceptance of others, in your personal contentment, in the demonstration of your servant's heart. Let them see you reading your Bible daily and hear your prayers for their faith. And by all means, don your towel and carry your basin as you live a life of service to those God brings across your path. You are the person of greatest influence on your offspring. Go forward, therefore, and be a faith influence for Jesus Christ in the next generation.

Please know that God always honors your faith nourishment of your family. You may not always see it or know of it, but God is at work in the life of your precious ones. Faith is being built by your example. Right now, I could be speaking to a Lois or a Eunice whose child or grandchild will grow to love the Lord with all his or her heart and soul and strength (Deut. 6:4). A higher calling is not known. A greater privilege is not available. Go ahead and sew a robe. "Train up a child in the way he should go, and when he is old he will not depart from it" (Prov. 22:6).

. . . faith comes from hearing the message and the message is heard through the word of Christ.
ROMANS 10:17

THE POINT TO FAITH

Train up a child in the way he should go, and when he is old he will not depart from it.
PROVERBS 22:6

Every child needs a personal faith trainer. You are it. Mothers trained in righteousness produce righteous-ready children. As you give attention to your relationship with God, you will provide an invaluable faith model for your child. Our society puts much emphasis on physical fitness, but I believe exercising our faith is the most important workout to which we should commit. Decide now to put your faith at the top of your priority list as well as your family's.

PRAYER: *Father in heaven, I ask You this day for wisdom to teach my children to walk in a way that pleases You. Help me to model faith in God in our home. Thank You for the privilege of encouraging faith in the next generation. In Jesus' Name I pray. Amen.*

PART II

Living Water

*Let anyone who is thirsty come to me and
drink. Whoever believes in me, as the
Scripture has said, rivers of living water will
flow from within them.*

JOHN 7:37-38

FAITH FEEDING 5

*. . . [Eli's] sons made themselves contemptible,
and he failed to restrain them.*

1 SAMUEL 3:13

BAD NEWS BOYS

THE STORY

(SEE GENESIS 35, 49; 1 KINGS 1; 1 SAMUEL 2, 3)

D
eep in the Bible is buried the story of some Bad News Boys whose antics had a lasting effect on their families and even the history of their nation. All of these sons had one thing in common: a father who withheld discipline.

As Bible history would have it, Jacob, the grandson of Abraham, was the patriarch of the Jewish nation. God actually gave Jacob the name *Israel* to signify his role as the father of his people. Jacob's twelve sons would become the foundation of the twelve tribes of Israel. Ideally, we would think that as a parent of such important sons, Jacob excelled in raising his boys in the way of the Lord. But, not so fast to assume! We only have to go as far as his firstborn to discover disobedience and rebellion. "While Israel was living in that region, Reuben went in and slept with his father's concubine, Bilhah, and Israel heard of it" (Gen. 35:22).

Jacob had many great qualities, but disciplining his sons was not one of them. The Scripture says that Israel "heard of it." It was a lifetime later, however, that he held Reuben accountable for this grievous and sinful act. Genesis 49 is an account of what would happen to the sons in the future. Listen to the words of Jacob to his firstborn. "Reuben, you are my firstborn, my might, the first sign of my strength, excelling in honor, excelling in power. Turbulent as the waters, you will no longer excel, for you went up onto your father's bed, onto my couch and defiled it" (Gen. 49:3-4). Oh, that Jacob had raised his son in the discipline of the Lord.

Where kings are concerned, there is none like King David. As an earthly king, he gave Israel her most prosperous years. David was a "man after God's own heart" (1 Sam. 13:14) and was blessed by God to be in the line of the future and eternal king, Jesus. Even David, however, was not without Bad News Boys. One of them was his third son, Absalom. The history of Absalom includes the murder of his brother and an effort to take over the kingship of Israel from his father. In addition, 1 Kings 1:6 sadly reports David's lack as one who did not hold his fourth son, Adonijah, accountable: "(His father had never interfered with him by asking, 'Why do you behave as you do?' He was also very handsome and born next after Absalom.)" It sounds to me like father David was swayed by the outward appearance of his son and skirted his responsibility as a parent.

Finally, there are Hophni and Phinehas, the sons of Eli, the priest. God describes Eli's sons as "wicked men with no regard for the Lord" (1 Sam. 2:12). As priests, they stole the meat meant for sacrifice to the Lord. God held them accountable for their sin even though their father did not. "For I told him that I would judge his family forever because of the sin he knew about; his sons made themselves contemptible, and he failed to restrain them" (1 Sam. 3:13).

These Bad News Boys brought shame and dishonor to their families and their country's history. Though they lived long ago, the lesson from their actions lives on today. Therein lies the beauty of the Bible's honesty and application to this day and age.

The Nourishment

. . . [Eli's] sons made themselves contemptible,
and he failed to restrain them.

1 Samuel 3:13

As a priest of God, Eli was held to a high standard. So, too, were his sons, Hophni and Phineas. However, in their greed and dishonesty, they misused the people's offerings. The Bible says in 1 Samuel 2:17, "This sin of the young men was very great in the Lord's sight for they were treating the Lord's offering with contempt." Not only were they dishonoring God through their priestly work, they were carrying on immoral lifestyles (1 Sam. 2:22). Eli knew about the sins of his sons and even spoke to them about it. His failure, however, to properly discipline his sons led to judgment against the line of Eli.

TELL THEM THE STORY OF ELI. EXPLAIN
THAT YOU AS THEIR PARENT ARE ACCOUNTABLE
TO YOUR HEAVENLY FATHER FOR THEM.

Godly parental restraint and discipline is the pathway of blessing for our children. The godly response to parental love and discipline is godly obedience. Eli's admonition from the Lord serves to remind us that we are accountable to God for the discipline we teach our children. Use this verse to remind your children of your responsibility as a godly parent to show them love tempered with godly discipline. Use everyday situations to highlight the importance of obedience. Tell them the story of Eli. Explain that you as their parent are accountable to your heavenly Father for them.

Here are six practical aspects of godly discipline:
- Pray daily for the wisdom, strength and patience to be a godly parent.
- Teach your child the expected standard of conduct as a member of your family.
- Teach your child to ask for specific forgiveness. "Please forgive me for (*fill in offense*)."
- Be consistent in your rebuke and punishment of the committed offense.
- Remind your child often of your love and responsibility as a godly parent.
- Daily model your obedient relationship to your heavenly Father.

As the Father has loved me, so I have loved you.
Now remain in my love. If you obey my commands,
you will remain in my love, just as I have
obeyed my Father's commands and remain in his love.
JOHN 15:9-10

THE LESSON

God used Eli mightily in the life of our friend, Hannah. He prayed for her to have a child when she had none, and Samuel was born. Then each year when Hannah took the robe she'd made to Samuel, Eli would bless Elkanah and Hannah, saying, "May the Lord give you children by this woman to take the place of the one she prayed for and gave to the Lord" (1 Sam. 2:20). In answer to Eli's annual prayer, Hannah had the children for which she longed. In addition, Eli was the one to whom Samuel was entrusted. In Eli's care, Samuel grew up in the presence of the Lord. And yet, this lesson revolves around Eli's inability to raise up his own sons to be godly priests.

The Bible also gives us insight on Samuel's two sons in 1 Samuel 8:2-3: "The name of [Samuel's] firstborn was Joel and the name of the second was Abijah, and they served at Beersheba. But his sons did not walk in his ways. They turned aside after dishonest gain and accepted bribes and perverted justice." It is hard to imagine that Eli and Samuel, such godly men, both fathered sons that dishonored God. The fact is that there are no guarantees regarding the outcome of the character of our children. That, however, does not alter in any way our responsibility as parents before God. As I said earlier, your place of influence carries two greats: great privilege and great responsibility. What is a mother to do?

To quote my little granddaughter, "I have a good idea!" Let's check the manual. Don't you wish kiddos came with a manual? It would cover topics such as what to expect and how to program. No doubt, there would be a whole section devoted to troubleshooting. Let's not be so fast to dismiss the idea of a manual. Actually, children do come with instructions. There is even a customer service number.

- **What to expect**—*Listen, my son, to your father's instruction and do not forsake your mother's teaching.*
  PROVERBS 1:8

- **How to program**—*These commands that I give you today are to be upon your hearts. Impress them on your children. Talk about them when you sit at home and when you walk along the road, when you lie down and when you get up.*
  DEUTERONOMY 6: 6-7

- **Troubleshooting**—*Ask and it will be given you; seek and you will find; knock and the door will be opened to you. For everyone who asks receives, he who seeks finds; to him who knocks the door will be opened.*
  LUKE 11:9-10

- **Customer service number**—*Call to me and I will answer*
you and tell you things you do not know.

JEREMIAH 33:3

The Bible manual is full of parenting guidelines and wisdom. As a young mother, I made a commitment to read the book of Proverbs. The Bible says, "King Solomon was greater in riches and wisdom than all the other kings of the earth. The whole world sought an audience with Solomon to hear the wisdom God had put in his heart" (1 Kings 10:23-24). I considered those words to be a good book promo and I wasn't disappointed. From Solomon I learned the practical framework of godly living. Proverbs gave me insight into the human heart and God's picture of righteous living. Gradually, I implemented Solomon's wisdom into my mothering and left the results to God. With 31 chapters, Proverbs lends itself to daily reading. You can cover the whole book in a month. Proverbs is a book of contrasts. It is apt reading for moms who live in a world of daily contrasts. Proverbs is a book of choices. Think about the choices your children face. Proverbs is a book of wisdom and understanding. Godly parenting demands both. Just think! You have at your fingertips what the whole world once sought—the God-given wisdom of Solomon. Don't delay. Hop on the Proverbs bandwagon!

Also within the Bible manual is the shortest parenting course ever. In only fifty-eight words, children and parents are given instructions that will reap eternal benefits if followed. In his letter to the church at Ephesus, the apostle Paul speaks to them about their relationships—with Jesus, with each other and within the family. Listen with me to his words:

Children, obey your parents in the Lord, for this is right. Honor your father and mother—which is the first commandment with a promise— that it may go well with you and that you may enjoy long life on earth. Fathers, do not exasperate your children; instead, bring them up in the training and instruction of the Lord.

EPHESIANS 6:1-4

Now let us consider together what these fifty-eight words mean to us as ones accountable to God for the godly parenting of our children.

THE COMMAND

Children obey your parents . . . honor your father and mother. In Exodus 20, God gave Moses the Ten Commandments. The first four commandments speak of our relationship to God. The fifth through the tenth speak of our relationships with others. The first of these last six is "Honor your father and mother, so that you may live long in the land the Lord is giving you." If this is the command from God that our children have been given, it is our duty as parents to do all we are able to help them keep it. Therein lies the essence of godly parenting. It is that important. Godly parenting is not driven by what we have, but by who we are. Faith crosses all socioeconomic, political, and racial lines. Faith in God is defined by God's Word as given to us in the Bible. Speaking God's Word into the lives of our children fosters the ability of our children to be obedient to commandment number five.

THE PROMISE

There are three reasons given for following this command. It is the right thing to do; if you do it, life will be good for you; "and that you may enjoy long life on earth." God's commands are always for our benefit. They are never given outside of God's love. They are always attainable within his power at work in us. "This is right" means that it is right according to God's desire for children. Doing what is right in God's eyes is the place of greatest blessing. Do we not all want that for our children, grandchildren, nieces, nephews, friends, and neighbor children? We want it because it is what God wants. ". . . that it may go well with you" is according to God's standard of well, not the world's standard. Well to God means blessed with peace and full of the joy and hope of the Lord. The world's well is based on success, possessions, and power. In God's well, your child may, indeed, also enjoy "worldly well," but it is not the primary aim of obedience to parents. ". . . enjoy long life on the earth" is God's ideal for his children. We know, however, that life today is anything but ideal. Because of sin, our world is tainted with life and joy-robbers such as illness, disease, violence, and immorality. As mothers we must trust God's sovereignty in the lives of our children. By his character and the giving of his Son, He has demonstrated his steadfast love and faithfulness. By faith we know that God loves our children even more than we do. By faith we entrust each of them to his eternal care.

THE CHALLENGE

"Fathers do not exasperate your children . . . " We are helped with the meaning of this verse by how Paul stated the same concept to the parents in his letter to the Colossians. "Children, obey your parents for this pleases the Lord. Fathers, do not embitter your children, or they will become discouraged" (Col. 3:20-21). In biblical times, discipline of children fell solely to the father. Today, however, mothers must also heed this admonishment. In many cases, mothers bear the sole responsibility for their children. In all instances, mothers, we are to encourage our children to honor their parents, "for this pleases the Lord." Godly parenting flourishes in a positive and encouraging home.

THE TASK

"Bring them up in the training and instruction of the Lord." We have come full circle, right back to Solomon's wisdom of Proverbs 22:6, our previous Faith Feeding principle. "Train up a child in the way he should go" is number one on our Growing Robe. I encourage you to find a group of like-minded mothers, either in your church or in your neighborhood or even in your workplace. Study together the scriptural principles of Faith Feeding. Pray for the faith of each other's children. Encourage one another to take responsibility for faith training in your homes. It is the work of the church to support the family in training and instruction of the Lord. However, do not rely on the church or default to it regarding teaching your own children. Your kids have your name on them where godly discipline is concerned. Teach your children to walk with God in a right relationship. Do so first by example. If necessary, use words and time outs!

There is benefit to keeping the fifth commandment beyond what is stated. There is a satisfaction and fulfillment that comes from being in right relationship with your heavenly Father by being in right relationship with your parents. Some time ago I noticed that a small basement window in the house next door was broken. Knowing that heavy rain was expected, I reported the broken window to my neighbor. She knew nothing of it. It was not until after her young son came home from school that he told her he had accidentally broken the window while playing ball in the playroom the afternoon before. Don't you know that this little guy had a restless night and day at school? Leverage your child's young conscience by encouraging obedience and respect that brings honor to you as a parent.

The psalmist, David, wise King Solomon's father, wrote a beautiful song about the richness of the Law of the Lord. His words are found in Psalm 19:7-11:

The law of the Lord is perfect, reviving the soul.
The statutes of the Lord are trustworthy, making wise the simple.
The precepts of the Lord are right, giving joy to the heart.
The commands of the Lord are radiant, giving light to the eyes.
The fear of the Lord is pure, enduring forever.
The ordinances of the Lord are sure and altogether righteous.
They are more precious than much pure gold;
They are sweeter than honey, than honey from the comb.
By them your servant is warned.
In keeping them there is great reward.

What is a mother to do? Heed these words; they are right out of the manual that came with your child. Hide them in your heart and pass them to your children. Eli knew the manual well. How grievous for

Hophni and Phineas that their earthly father didn't hold them accountable to their heavenly Father's decrees. Lord, enable us to be women of godly influence in the next generation.

Be imitators of God, therefore, as dearly loved children and live
a life of love, just as Christ loved us and gave himself up for us as a
fragrant offering and sacrifice to God.
EPHESIANS 5:1

THE POINT TO FAITH

[Eli's] sons made themselves contemptible,
and he failed to retrain them.
1 SAMUEL 3:13

Does your own corrective tone reverberate in your ears when your head hits the pillow at night? Discipline can be exhausting. It can also appear to be ineffective when you are in the middle of it. Godly discipline requires a healthy understanding of the precepts of the Bible. It also requires a consistent and cumulative approach. Stress the importance of behavior in light of eternity. Connect their actions today with their hopes of tomorrow. And pray that when your children are adult parents, three words spoken by their dear mother will reverberate in their ears: Obedience brings blessing.

PRAYER: *Dear Jesus, help me to be a mother who disciplines my children in love. Give me grace when I am weary and peace when I feel stress. I am grateful for your patience with me as I learn to obey your commands. Enable me to teach my children principles of faith. In Jesus' Name I pray. Amen.*

FAITH FEEDING 6

"Do all that you have in mind,"
his armor-bearer said.
"Go ahead; I am with you heart and soul."

1 SAMUEL 14:7

CLIFF CLIMBING

THE STORY

(1 SAMUEL 14:1-23)

In the era of the ancient history of the nation of Israel, it was the Philistines who were the greatest threat. The Philistines loomed large in stature and in their hatred of the followers of the one true God.

In the early days of King Saul, "the Philistines assembled to fight Israel with three thousand chariots, six thousand charioteers, and soldiers as numerous as the sand on the seashore" (1 Sam. 13:5). The king's son, Jonathan, set out without his father's knowledge to a Philistine outpost. The Bible says, "One day Jonathan son of Saul said to the young man bearing his armor, "Come, let us go over to the Philistine outpost on the other side" (1 Sam. 14:1). It was a crazy idea, one would think, to separate yourself from the army and meet the enemy as a pair. The armor-bearer may have been thinking in terms of our current lingo: *What is he thinking?* Nevertheless, they set out on their mission to the outpost. Notice, I said, "their mission." Such was the role of an armor-bearer. Jonathan's mission was his mission. The story relates the wholehearted service of the armor-bearer to his master. Listen to this story of the partnership between the son of King Saul and the young man bearing his armor.

> *Jonathan said to his young armor-bearer,*
> *"Come, let us go over to the outpost of those uncircumcised fellows.*
> *Perhaps the Lord will act in our behalf. Nothing can hinder*
> *the Lord from saving, whether by many or by few."*
> *"Do all that you have in mind," his armor-bearer said.*
> *"Go ahead, I am with you heart and soul."*
> 1 SAMUEL 14:6-7

As the account continues, it becomes obvious that the young armor-bearer's allegiance and cooperation were well placed. God, indeed, was with them that day, and they had success as two against many. Their outpost victory, which seemed isolated from the rest of the army, actually caused a panic in the Philistine army that led to confusion and their defeat. "So the Lord rescued Israel that day" (1 Sam. 14:23).

Jonathan's armor-bearer may not have volunteered for the job, but he certainly embraced the job he was assigned. Being the armor-bearer to the king's son was an honor. What strikes me about this young man is his wholehearted devotion to Jonathan's mission. He trusted Jonathan's wisdom and had confidence in Jonathan's God. In his heart he knew the outcome and was willing to put his life on the line for it.

God used the conquest of the Philistine outpost by a man and a boy for his own purposes. It took the pair of them to accomplish the task. On his stone pillow at the end of the day, Jonathan would have thanked God for the words of his armor-bearer, "Go ahead, do all that you have in mind. I am with you heart and soul." (Translation: Carry on! I am with you all the way.)

THE NOURISHMENT

"Do all that you have in mind,"
his armor-bearer said. "Go ahead;
I am with you heart and soul."

1 SAMUEL 14:7

Let your children know for certain that you are supportive of them in their growing years. Affirm their ideas when they reflect their gifts and show wisdom. Assure them that God's plan and purpose for them will prevail.

Be an armor-bearer for your child by embracing their ideas as they grow. There is nothing that gives more encouragement than someone else to share your mission. By making your child's mission *your mission,* you validate his or her hopes and dreams. You make a strong statement that you are a proactive participant in their life. Taking on their ideas and sharing their passion affirms their gifts. With you on their side, they are likely to give their best effort.

REMIND THEM OFTEN THAT YOU WILL COOPERATE WITH GOD'S PLAN FOR THEIR LIVES. THIS REQUIRES TRUST IN YOUR CHILD'S PERSPECTIVE AND HIS OR HER OWN EVALUATION OF WHAT IS BEST.

Teach your offspring to expect God to speak through them. Remind them often that you will cooperate with God's plan for their lives. This requires trust in your child's perspective and his or her own evaluation of what is best. This wholehearted willingness to flank them also requires your trust in the Lord and an active prayer life on your child's behalf.

By being their armor-bearer, you will share their successes and their failures. What could be better than a mother who really understands the challenges you have met in your young life?

Often, I think of a man who graduated with degrees in a specialized course of science. On one of his trips to his home, he discovered informational books about his area of study on his mother's bookshelf. When he inquired about what led her to read such material, his mother simply replied, "I wanted to have some understanding of what you were facing and learning. It has made me appreciate your hard work even more." I could see in this son's face as he relayed this story his appreciation of a mother who was with him all the way.

Just remember: Being an armor-bearer for your son or daughter is about what *they* have in mind. Being with them heart and soul requires a yielded spirit on your part. As you allow them to take the lead, they will be increasingly willing to trust your input. Like the story of Jonathan and his armor-bearer, the story of the partnership between you and your child will go down through the ages—perhaps even to your grandchildren.

For I am the LORD, your God, who takes hold of your right hand
and says to you, "Do not fear; I will help you."
ISAIAH 41:13

THE LESSON

At the heart of the relationship between the armor-bearer and Jonathan was a mutual trust in God. The armor-bearer's wholehearted response to Jonathan went beyond duty and even beyond friendship. Jonathan's servant believed in Jonathan's plan because he believed in Jonathan's God. Together they formed a team against their common enemy. Together they made a historical difference. The Philistines were an arch-enemy of Israel.

Therefore, they were an enemy of God. The Bible says that "Israel has become a stench to the Philistines" (1 Sam. 13:4) and that "all the troops . . . were quaking with fear" (1 Sam. 13:7). Yet, Jonathan asked his armor-bearer to climb a high cliff and fight the enemy as two against many. He said to him, "Climb up after me; the Lord has given them into the hands of Israel" (1 Sam. 14:12). And so they climbed up the cliff together, and together they met the enemy face to face. Indeed, God did give them victory. The two against twenty prevailed. And God did more. He used their courage spurred by faith to rout the enemy. "Then panic struck the whole army . . . it was a panic sent by God" (1 Sam. 14:15). Eventually, the panic turned to total confusion in the Philistine army. "They found the Philistines in total confusion, striking each other with their swords" (1 Sam. 14:20). God used an unlikely team—a king's son and his assigned servant— to accomplish his will. Would Jonathan have been so courageous if the armor-bearer had said, "No way, man! You are a fool. I refuse to help you!"? The armor-bearer's belief in the presence of God within Jonathan made all the difference that day.

Have you ever had someone believe in you? If so, you know the value of partnership. Spiritual partnership with your child will make a significant difference in your child's life. It is a beautiful moment when a mother comes to the realization that God is present and working in her child's heart and mind. In that moment, a mother's response is crucial to her son or daughter's independence from her and their dependence on God. As it was for Jonathan and his armor-bearer, it is an "outpost moment" that you do not want to miss. It is a robe to grow into for your child. "Go ahead, do all that you have in mind; I am with you heart and soul" is a message of hope. It tells your young person that you value their wisdom and their courage. It puts you on their team. It is an affirmation of God's hand on their plans. The outcome is paled by the faith response from a faith mother to a faith child. Your heart and soul commitment is a "yes" heard deep in the heart and soul of the one to whom you gave life. I ask you, what could be better than that?

I believe Jonathan knew the armor-bearer's response before he asked for a commitment to such a courageous act. He'd witnessed his servant's cooperation and wholehearted support before he arrived at the cliffs of Bozez and Seneh that day. For your child, perhaps the "yes" moments from Mom began with a lemonade stand on the corner, a daily catch in the back yard, or baking cupcakes to give to a friend. Perhaps it started with a science project or a golf lesson. Your child's desire to give food or warm blankets to the homeless may have gotten your attention. Belief in your child is expressed in increments over time—consistent and cumulative increments. As you earn their trust, they will know it is safe to share with you their need for a partner in what God has laid on their heart to do.

God has graced my own life with "yes" moments with my children. Looking back I see that they were like rungs of a ladder leading to a higher place of trust in God for each of them. When my daughter was a senior in high school, she made a decision that at the time was outside of herself. After being encouraged by winning a voice competition, she decided to compete for a voice scholarship at a college that had an excellent reputation in music. I can still picture her as she sat on the window seat in our kitchen. And I can still hear the confidence in her words, "This is what I am going to do . . . "

"Go ahead," I replied. "Do all that you have in mind. I am with you heart and soul." It was a "yes" opportunity of a lifetime for me. My "yes" overrode any looming doubts in her mind. My words strengthened her confidence. They set her securely on the path that was before her. The rest was up to the Lord. I was right behind her when she climbed the cliff. At every turn of her college career, I was there to remind her of what she'd had in mind that day. And it was so—all that she had in mind.

Another "yes" occasion came for me a few years later with my son. He called from college one day and said, "Are you sitting down? I have prayed about something I want to tell you." Immediately, I did two things. I sat down and put my hand over my mouth lest I would speak too quickly in response and refute his answer to prayer. "I love biology (his present major—three years in), but I have a passion for languages." Thank the Lord that his news was no surprise to me. I had perceived the shift in his heart since his return from a foreign study term. My husband and I were able to visit him in Spain and watch his passion for languages unfurl.

"I am with you all the way, son." I was cliff climbing again and trusting the Lord with every advance. And it was so—all that he had in mind.

As mothers, we will be touched by a biblical example of God's use of a pair of like-minded relatives. Their armor-bearer account is written for us by Dr. Luke (Luke 1). The story of their mutual trust in God goes like this:

Once upon a BC century in a small town in the hill country of Judea when Herod was king, God spoke to a man named Zechariah. Zechariah was a priest of the Lord. He was married to a woman who was also in the priestly lineage of Aaron. Zechariah and Elizabeth lived as a God-fearing and God-pleasing couple. Life was good for them except that Elizabeth was barren. As we learned from Elkanah and Hannah, failure to have an heir was considered a disgrace in those days. Thank the Lord, however, that unlike Elkanah, Zechariah was the husband of only one wife. And so it came to pass that while Zechariah was completing his priestly duty at the prescribed time, an angel of the Lord visited him. Actually, the angel startled Zechariah. And what the angel had to say dumbfounded the old priest.

"Do not be afraid, Zechariah; your prayer has been heard. Your wife Elizabeth will bear you a son, and you are to give him the name John" (Luke 1:13). What an angel of the Lord says always comes to pass and, yes, Elizabeth became pregnant with Zechariah's child. Weren't they a joyous couple?

Elizabeth expressed her gratitude to God, "The Lord has done this for me . . . In these days he has shown favor and taken away my disgrace among the people" (Luke 1:25). The truth is that the Lord had done more than grant her favor and remove her disgrace. He had given her a son who would be the most important herald the world has ever known. He would prepare the way for another child. This child would be born to her virgin relative, Mary. Mary's child would be named Jesus, and He would save God's people from their sins.

Elizabeth was six months into her pregnancy when the angel of the Lord made another conception announcement. This time the angel visited the young virgin who was pledged to a man named Joseph. The angel's words to Mary startled her as well. "Do not be afraid, Mary, you have found favor with God. You will be with child and give birth to a son, and you are to give him the name Jesus" (Luke 1:30-31). Mary questioned the angel as to how it could be that she would have a child since she was a virgin.

The angel answered, "The Holy Spirit will come upon you, and the power of the Most High will overshadow. So the holy one to be born will be called the Son of God. Even Elizabeth your relative is going to have a child in her old age, and she who was said to be barren is in her sixth month. "For nothing is impossible with God" (Luke 1:35-37).

I do not know how much of that conversation with Gabriel Mary took in, but I bet the news about Elizabeth's ability to bear a child sealed the deal in her young mind. Mary answered with words that were outside of herself, "I am the Lord's servant. May it be to me as you have said" (Luke 1:38).

Once upon a time in a BC century, the mother-to-be in the hill country town of Judea received a visit from the mother-to-be from Nazareth. Both expected sons, and both sons were miracle babies. The Scriptures describing the meeting of the expectant mothers is so riveting that you should hear them as written. "When Elizabeth heard Mary's greeting, the baby leaped in her womb, and Elizabeth was filled with the Holy Spirit. In a loud voice she exclaimed: 'Blessed are you among women, and blessed is the child you will bear! Blessed is she who has believed that the Lord would fulfill his promises to her!'" (Luke 1:41-42, 45).

At that moment in a BC century, Mary received from God just what she needed to climb the cliff that was before her—an armor-bearer in the person of her relative. How good is God? Elizabeth believed the unbelievable in Mary before it was ever spoken. "Go ahead, Mary, do all that you have in mind. I am with you heart and soul."

I think as mothers we would all agree that the cliff that Mary climbed was the most difficult motherhood cliff ever faced. She served Almighty God by being a vessel of humanity for his Son. Her son served humanity by being a vessel of salvation for the world. He willingly gave his life for those that Mary would never know on this earth—you and me. Thank God for Mary and her armor-bearer.

Armor-bearers are in great demand. Will you be one? Do you need one? Come on, I'll be right behind you. I am with you all the way!

> *. . . the one who is in you is*
> *greater than the one who is in the world.*
> 1 JOHN 4:4

THE POINT TO FAITH

> *"Do all that you have in mind," his armor-bearer said.*
> *"Go ahead: I am with you heart and soul."*
> 1 SAMUEL 14:7

The world that our children face is increasingly volatile and risky. Who better to carry their shield and sword than the one who has birthed them and nurtured them? You know their strengths and their weaknesses, their hopes and dreams. Your own past experience tells you they will need all the support they can garner to do all that they have in mind. Your belief in their intrinsic value makes you an excellent candidate for an armor-bearer. Go for it, mother!

PRAYER: *Lord, You know well the value of having a mother who cooperates with God's plan. Your own mother knew of your divine origin and purpose even though she didn't know all the details of your life. Show me how to come alongside my children every day so that they can fulfill your plan in their lives. In faith, I accept this role. In faith, I trust You to encourage and enable those in my care to realize their deepest desires and dreams according to your will. In Jesus' Name I pray. Amen.*

*And who knows but that you have
come to your royal position for such a time as this?*

ESTHER 4:14

HADASSAH'S STORY— GOD'S GLORY

THE STORY

(SEE BOOK OF ESTHER)

As I stood in the courtyard of the ancient Moorish castle Alhambra in Granada, Spain, I was transported to another time and place. This was not the palace of King Xerxes but certainly much like it. The king's chambers were down a corridor on my right, and there before me was The Myrtle Court on the main level; a series of small rooms lined the outside limits of the second floor. I stood breathless as I surveyed the balcony rooms. It was as though I could see the young Jewess named Hadassah being served by her attendants. I could easily imagine her receiving beauty treatments, eating specially prepared meals of meat and protein, and glowing as a woman with assurance of her identity.

Hadassah lived in the citadel of Susa in one of the 127 provinces over which King Xerxes ruled. In Susa, Hadassah "was also known as Esther"

(Esther 2:7), her Persian name. Mordecai, who was Esther's cousin, served as her parent when she became orphaned. He honored his uncle's memory and sure intentions by raising Esther according to Jewish tradition and faith in the one true God. This upbringing was not easy in Babylonia, the place to which they had been exiled.

The book of Esther introduces us to an unhappy King Xerxes, who was displeased with his wife, Queen Vashti, and soon banished her. The king's personal attendant suggested a search for beautiful young virgins for the king, and he agreed. No hard decision there! Esther 2:7 says that Esther was "lovely in form and features" and that she was entrusted to Hegai, who was in charge of the king's harem. It is no surprise that this young and most beautiful girl pleased Hegai and won his favor. Actually, Esther 2:15 says, "Esther won the favor of everyone who saw her." Most importantly, "the king was attracted to Esther more than any of the other women, and she won his favor and approval more than any of the other virgins. So he set a royal crown on her head and made her queen instead of Vashti" (Esther 2:17). Into the drab and cold cement edifice Esther brought untold beauty, radiant light, and a soon-to-be-revealed mission with eternal significance.

Esther's beauty won favor with the king, and her heart won favor with God. The story of Esther is one of risk, courage, and faith. At the end of the day, God used her physical and heart beauty to save the lives of the Jews under King Xerxes' authority. Her efforts foiled a plot to destroy all the Jews in the land and led to the death of the one who tried to have Mordecai and his people annihilated. Subsequently, Esther saved her people, and Mordecai became second in command to King Xerxes. More importantly, God preserved His people, the Jews, through the beauty, courage, and wisdom of one woman. An annual day to honor Esther is still celebrated today. It is called the Day of Purim.

The Jewess named Hadassah, renamed Esther, brought God's light inside the king's palace. She was in the right place at the right time, and God used her mightily. Hadassah's story—God's glory, indeed!

THE NOURISHMENT

And who knows but that you have
come to your royal position for such a time as this?
ESTHER 4:14

The story of Esther is one of beauty and adventure on the surface. A closer look finds this story to be anything but a fairytale. Esther is a young woman who was cast into compromise and risk. King Xerxes' palace is the last place you would want your daughter to live as a young woman. God was with Esther, however, and used her beauty and attractiveness to the king to accomplish a mighty work for His people. Esther's royal position defined her mission in life. She courageously embraced her opportunity to influence the king for God's purposes. Esther was reminded of God's hand in her life and his plan for her by the words of Mordecai (Esther 4:12-14). He helped her overcome her fear and to trust God with the results. Mostly, Mordecai communicated to Esther God's affirmation of the task. It was like Mordecai was saying, "This is yours to do. It has your name on it, Hadassah Esther." In hindsight, Esther's entrance into the king's sphere of influence was neither casual nor frivolous.

The truth is that a life of faith is full of royal positions. These are times and situations decreed by God to accomplish a specific outcome in our lives and the lives of our children. Recognizing our royal positions is a key to understanding the value of each season on our life calendar.

"For such a time as this." These words communicate the value of mission in your child's life. They help instill the principle of intentional living. Such an approach will connect effort with outcome and help your child gain confidence as each plateau is reached. Also, it encourages you and your child to work toward specific goals and through challenges. In the process, they learn to focus on what they deem important, build on their successes, and learn from their failures. They also develop discernment

about what is theirs to do, what has their name on it. The goal is to be able
to identify their royal position for such a time as this and to accept it as a
season of growth and meaning.

HELP YOUR CHILDREN TO RECOGNIZE SPECIFIC
SEASONS IN THEIR YOUNG LIVES: SEASONS OF FUN,
SEASONS OF CHALLENGE, SEASONS OF SUFFERING,
SADNESS, AND DISCIPLINE, SEASONS OF GROWTH,
AND SEASONS OF OPPORTUNITY.

Help your children to recognize specific seasons in their young lives:
seasons of fun, seasons of challenge, seasons of suffering, sadness, and
discipline, seasons of growth, and seasons of opportunity. Teach them
that each season is filtered through God's hand and that they can trust
their heavenly Father to guide and help them through whatever the present holds. Ask questions like: How does this situation make you feel?
What is God trying to teach us? How can you shine God's light in this
situation? How should we pray for God's help?

Encountering stumbling blocks is a reality of childhood (and every
other stage of "hood"). Stumbling blocks may enter their path from well-
meaning or not-so-well-meaning individuals. They may arise from limited
resources and abilities. Often, a child is held back by his own feelings of
insufficiency. It is difficult to watch your loved one struggle with obstacles
that challenge their everyday life. As you raise awareness of the concept
of viewing seasons of life as royal positions, I encourage you to teach your
children that stumbling blocks are mere stepping-stones. As in a swiftly
flowing creek, stepping-stones will take us to the other side. And what
is more, God will use the stumbling blocks turned stepping-stones to
strengthen the character and faith of our vulnerable children. Just remember, in God's economy, stumbling blocks are never wasted!

TEACH YOUR CHILDREN THAT STUMBLING BLOCKS ARE MERE STEPPING STONES.

Teach your children that stumbling blocks are mere stepping stones. When you regularly speak the words *for such a time as this,* your children will learn to recognize the value of their current life condition and the opportunity to make the most of each season of their lives.

Take note: This Faith Feeding principle aptly applies to mothers as well. What is your present royal position? I pray that you will be filled with God's Spirit for such a time as this.

There is a time for everything,
and a season for every activity under heaven.
ECCLESIASTES 3:1

THE LESSON

The story of Esther is enchanting and exciting. It reads like a fairytale. A young Jewish woman is invited to live in the king's palace because of her beauty. She is given twelve months of luxurious beauty treatments and excellent food. She not only has personal servants but also a personal trainer. In due course of time, she meets the king and he is wowed enough by her to make her queen and hold a great celebration in her honor. To top it off, the king proclaimed a royal edict: "He proclaimed a holiday throughout the provinces and distributed gifts with royal liberality" (Esther 2:18). We can imagine that as the news of Esther's royal position spread throughout Xerxes's kingdom, all the little girls gave themselves over to a dream to have a life just like Queen Esther. And you thought princess gowns were just a current trend!

To understand the impact of Queen Esther on King Xerxes, we must draw from the history of the Jewish nation. Through Abraham, God brought forth a people that were distinguishable as his own. They became a nation of people who believe in one God. God called them *Israel*. Their story is told in the Old Testament of the Bible beginning in Genesis 12. Eventually, Israel was taken over by the Babylonians. They were removed from their homeland and taken to the provinces of Babylon, one of which was Susa, where we find Mordecai and Esther for such a time as this. Most of the nation of Israel had previously forgotten their covenant with the one true God. The Bible says, however, that there was a remnant of worshippers of God. Mordecai's family, including Esther, was part of that remnant of believers.

Esther 2:5 tells us that Mordecai, from the tribe of Benjamin, had been carried into exile from Jerusalem by Nebuchadnezzar king of Babylon. It was dangerous for a Jew who worshipped one God to be in a land that worshipped many gods and idols. That danger surfaced in the king's palace in the person of Haman who was given a seat of honor by King Xerxes. Haman was the highest-ranking noble in the land. It was a law that all citizens were to bow down to Haman when in his presence. It was a command that Mordecai refused to obey. He refused to bow down to anyone but God. It was known that Mordecai belonged to a people who were foreign to the Babylonians. "Then Haman said to King Xerxes, 'There is a certain people dispersed among the peoples in all the provinces of your kingdom who keep themselves separate. Their customs are different from those of all other people, and they do not obey the king's laws; it is not in the king's best interest to tolerate them'" (Esther 3:8). This report from Haman to the king resulted in a decree that all the people of Mordecai's kind would be executed on a certain future date. We can quickly grasp the danger surrounding Queen Esther. Her story relates her obedience to her cousin, her faith in God, and her success in saving the remnant of the Most High God.

ESTHER'S OBEDIENCE

"Esther had not revealed to the king her nationality and family background because Mordecai had forbidden her to do so" (Esther 2:10). Mordecai was wise to tell Esther to be silent about her roots, and Esther was wise to obey him. If she had not, the king would have had her removed as soon as he heard Haman's side of the story. King Xerxes had already shown his penchant for quick action against those who did not obey the king's decrees. Early in the book of Esther, we read that Queen Vashti was removed permanently from the king's presence because of her disregard for the king's command. Because Esther honored Mordecai, who had become as a father to Esther, she remained in the palace where God could use her against Haman's plan.

ESTHER'S FAITH

The king's edict, sent to all the king's provinces, was "the order to destroy, kill and annihilate all the Jew—young and old, women and little children—on a single day" (Esther 3:13). Mordecai knew that without intervention by Esther, that edict would be carried out, and the remnant of God's people would be no more. Esther saw her mission clearly. She understood her cousin's message: "'Do not think that because you are in the king's house you alone of all the Jews will escape. For if you remain silent at this time, relief and deliverance will arise from another place, but you and your father's family will perish. And who knows but that you have come to royal position for such a time as this'" (Esther 4:13-14). Esther should not remain silent, but it was known that no one was to approach the king unless summoned. To do so could result in death. This called for a fast. Her message to Mordecai: "Go, gather together all the Jews who are in Susa, and fast for me. Do not eat or drink for three days, night or day. I and my attendants will fast as you do. When this is done, I will go to the king, even though it is against the law. And if I perish, I perish'" (Esther 4:16). It is noteworthy that Esther's faith is steadfast considering the fact that Esther is the only book in the Bible that does not mention the word *God*.

ESTHER'S SUCCESS

"On the third day, Esther put on her royal robes and stood in the court of the palace, in front of the king's hall. The king was sitting on his royal throne in the hall, facing the entrance. When he saw Queen Esther standing in the court, he was pleased with her and held out to her the gold scepter that was in his hand. So Esther approached and touched the tip of the scepter. Then the king asked, 'What is it, Queen Esther? What is your request? Even up to half the kingdom it will be given you'" (Esther 5:1-3). For such a time as this, the unmentioned God placed the beautiful Hadassah in the enemy camp and brought her out as a queen for all times in Jewish history.

Mordecai was right. Esther had come to royal position for such a time as this. "Who knows?" he'd asked. The Lord knows. He knew then, and He knows now. Furthermore, He knows forever. The Lord knew Esther's obedient heart. He knew the extent of her faith. The Lord used her obedience and her faith to give her success. There are two things to remember: Whatever your royal position, He knows it. Whatever your royal position, He will use your obedience and faith to bring you success in it. Wherever you are in life, face it with confidence and strength in the Lord. He does not bring us to royal position to expose our own weakness. He brings royal positions to us to prove His strength in us and to build our faith and godly character.

My husband and I have shared a unique and privileged royal position. We have been caregivers in our home to both my mother and his father. No doubt our dual caregiving was a commitment beyond ourselves. We thank God for our parents' sound minds and their kind and cooperative dispositions in their royal positions. We also thank God for the grace He has given us to care for our elders in a daily and personal way. At the time of this writing, my precious father-in-law is home with the Lord. He passed away at the age of 103. At the time of his departure, I sensed an unexpected wave of peace that came from knowing that we had done the right thing on his behalf. For such a time as this, our caregiving continues with my mother, who is now 92 years old. As I reflect on our caregiving season, I am deeply aware of God's continual grace in my life. Indeed, as the Lord told the apostle Paul, "My grace is sufficient for you, for my power is made perfect in weakness" (2 Cor. 12:9).

Early in this season, when I saw firsthand the confinement of it, I asked the Lord what He wanted me to accomplish in it. His answer was clear to me. *Serve me where you are right now.* I took His answer to heart by using my royal position for ministry to my elders and the mothers on my street. While I have been close at home in caring for our elders, God has given me close-to-home ministry. Our greatest challenge is to not be compromised in our desire to keep our children and grandchildren a priority in our lives. God has given them extensive grace toward our mission. They have demonstrated honor to their grandparents by their support. They are like Mordecai at the king's gate as they show concern for our welfare. Our whole family is engaged in our royal position. It is truly a blessing in our lives to see the little ones build relationships with their great-grandparents. Our home is rich in heritage for such a time as this. I ponder God's purposes. Could it be that I became a dual caregiver to become an author? We thank God for our royal position.

What "such a time as this" are you in right now? My heart tells me that your present royal position may be far more challenging than mine. Perhaps you are a single parent, an ill parent, a grieving parent, a depressed parent, or even a devastated parent. The possibilities of the seasons of your life are exhaustive. Thankfully, your God is not. There is no end to his grace and power. Your God is sovereign. Your God loves you. Your God will never leave you or forsake you. Your God is Esther's God. Like Esther, your position is royal. Your God is King. Your God reigns! "The one who calls you is faithful and he will do it" (1 Thess. 5:24).

I have heard it said that on the Feast of Purim day, which celebrates the deliverance of the Jews from the hand of the wicked Haman, the young girls don pretty dresses in honor of Esther. One thing is known for certain. The story of Esther is no tale of make believe. Rather it is a tale of the faith of Hadassah. It is a tale of the glory she brought to God in the royal position decreed by God. Give yourself over to the dream of a life like Esther's and make a difference in your own "such a time as this." The book of Esther is a fascinating account. Take time to read it for yourself!

> *For the Jews it was a time of happiness*
> *and joy, gladness and honor.*
> ESTHER 8:16

THE POINT TO FAITH

> *And who knows but that you have*
> *come to your royal position for such a time as this.*
> ESTHER 4:14

Life in the front end of the twenty-first century seems so random and disconnected. One minute we bring a baby home from the hospital, the next minute we take boy or girl to college. In between, there is myriad activity. But know this: There is no random in God. He knows every tick of earth's clock. Every movement is in direction toward God or away from Him. Teach your child, therefore, that every situation is a place to be used by God. Every season provides an opportunity to grow in the knowledge of God. Who knows what royal position you will face today? The Lord knows.

PRAYER: *Heavenly Father, I confess that the seasons of my life seem to be anything but royal. Give me eyes to see the importance of where I am right now. Also help me to instill in my child the need to embrace the seasons of their lives so that they grow in faith in one royal position after another. In Jesus' Name I pray. Amen.*

I have no greater joy than to hear
that my children are walking in the truth.

3 JOHN 1:4

NICK'S NIGHT JOB

THE STORY

(SEE JOHN 3:1-21)

When Nicodemus left his place at the city gate of Jerusalem, he didn't know that his name would take on new meaning that night. His name means conqueror of the people. As a Pharisee of high standing and a member of the Jewish ruling council, he believed that the way to conquer the people for God was through the Law of Moses—learn it, live it, teach it, and unfortunately, add to it. On his way home, his day job came in conflict with his night job. He met the One who conquers people with love.

As rigid as Nicodemus was as a teacher of the Law, he had softness in his heart that made him open to the true work of God. Acknowledging Jesus as a teacher who was from God was not a problem for Nicodemus. He had no trouble calling Jesus *Rabbi*. But to call Jesus the *Son of God* was another story. Unlike his colleagues, however, he could not dismiss the miracles that Jesus was performing. Thought of these miracles consumed him. In the last few weeks, it was all he could think about. He daydreamed about coming face to face with Jesus and asking Him how someone could do all these things if He were *not* the Son of God. "My thoughts must stay my thoughts," I imagine Nicodemus said to himself. He was an aristocrat. It was too risky to his career and his life to breathe a word of his questions out loud to anyone and most especially to Jesus. He would be excommunicated from his religion if it were known that this doubt about the kingdom of God and the law had pricked his soul. To the religious experts of the day, it would have been treason and blasphemy.

What Nicodemus didn't know was that the rabbi who so intrigued him already knew his thoughts and questions. And what's more, Nicodemus didn't know that his questions had come up on God's divine calendar. Not able to contain his curiosity, Nicodemus went to Jesus one night and asked his questions. Jesus' response led to a miracle in Nicodemus's heart. It was one thing to see Jesus heal people from their diseases and cast out demons. It was quite something else to have his own heart healed. One question led to another, and before the night was over, Nicodemus went from being a keeper of the Law to having Jesus in his heart for keeps.

Born again, Nicodemus was thrust into the kingdom of God that night. His night job began to take seed in his life. He had meaning and purpose that he'd never known in his day job. He found himself with a new courage. He even surprised himself at the next Jewish Council meeting when all the Jews were looking for a way to eliminate Jesus. Nicodemus stood right up and spoke to them about justice concerning Jesus. They didn't listen to him, but in his heart he knew he had changed. One can only imagine the consuming thoughts of Nicodemus on the night he went with another secret disciple of Jesus, Joseph of Arimathea, to give Jesus a proper burial according to Jewish custom.

The Bible records two times that Nicodemus went to Jesus at night: the night when he questioned Jesus and the night when he buried Jesus. The second was evidence of the first. Indeed, Jesus knew the heart of this man named Nicodemus. Indeed, Nicodemus came to know the heart of Jesus as well. It was never about the Law. It was always about the One who fulfilled the Law—Jesus, the God of the day and the night. At the end of the day, the Jewish legalist knew the whole Truth and nothing but the Truth. And the Truth is that the Name and love of Jesus conquers all.

THE NOURISHMENT

I have no greater joy than to hear
that my children are walking in the truth.

3 JOHN 1:4

Is your faith growing as you hear the Word of God in *Faith Feedings*? Romans 10:17 says, "Faith comes from hearing the message, and the message is heard through the word about Christ." On the night that Nicodemus met Jesus, he heard a clear message from Jesus. The Word of Christ to Nicodemus is the message of the Bible: "For God so loved the world that he gave his one and only Son, that whoever believes in him shall not perish but have eternal life" (John 3:16). The faith of Nicodemus brought Jesus great joy that night. He came to earth to show God's love to the world. Nicodemus believed in Jesus and received God's love gift, eternal life. There was rejoicing in heaven that night!

What brings us joy changes as our faith grows. The greatest joy to a mother of faith is a child of faith. Jesus expressed his thoughts about the faith of children in Mark 10:14-15. Jesus said, "Let the little children come to me, and do not hinder them, for the kingdom of God belongs to such as these. I tell you the truth, anyone who will not receive the kingdom of God like a little child will not enter it." Children have a great propensity for faith. Their hearts are full of trust, and they are willing to believe in Jesus and accept God's love. Nicodemus' heart was like a child's.

Children are never too young to hear the message of the Bible. In order to speak God's love into the lives of my young grandchildren, I have given each of them a small Bible. On the page where John 3:16 is found, I affixed a card with their picture on it. On the card I wrote: "God loves (*their name*)." Before they can read, write, or speak in compound sentences, they know the main point of the Bible—God loves me! What joy it brings me to see them open their Bible and "read" that God loves them. Every faith feeding that follows is built on the knowledge of God's love.

The fullness of faith is reflected in the greatest motherhood joy—to hear that your children are walking in the Truth. Make it your priority to communicate to your child that it is your greatest desire that they have Jesus in their heart. Pray that God will give you opportunity to share the Nick's Night Job truth with your child—"Very truly I tell you, no one can see the kingdom of God unless they are born again" (John 3:3).

In reality, all that you do as a faith-building mother prepares the soil of your child's heart to receive Jesus as their personal Lord and Savior. On a day of God's designing and choosing, He will prompt your son or daughter through his Holy Spirit to accept his gift of eternal life. How glad you will be to have cooperated with God's plan of salvation for your precious ones. These words also affirm your presence in the lives of children outside of your family. Do you volunteer in your church nursery? Are you a teacher in Sunday school, vacation Bible school, confirmation, or a catechism class? Perhaps you are a youth group leader, a mentor, or a children's choir director. At the very least, you have contact with young family members and the friends of your children. Make it your life mission to cultivate the soil of young hearts and minds. Post a yellow sticky on your mirror that reminds you to sow and water for Jesus! Above all else, pray continually for the children in your circle of influence.

REMIND THEM OFTEN AS THEY GROW OF THE TIME AND PLACE WHEN THEY GAVE THEIR HEART TO JESUS.

The earlier your child asks Jesus into their heart, the easier it will be for them to begin a heart relationship with God. When the time is right, say to your child, "Would you like to invite Jesus to live in your heart?" then ask them to repeat this simple prayer, phrase by phrase: "Dear Jesus, I am sorry for my sins. Please forgive me and come into my heart to live. I want to be with you forever. In Jesus' Name I pray, Amen." This prayer is basic and simple for a small child. It is concise and can be remembered by them as the specific time when they asked Jesus into their heart. I suggest that you write the prayer out and date it. Make it a marker in their life. Remind them often as they grow of the time and place when they gave their heart to Jesus. And rejoice, Mother, in their heart for God. It is a gift of God to you.

As their faith grows, so too will your joy. Do not delay. Ask motherhood's most privileged question—Would you like to invite Jesus into your heart? And leave the rest up to Jesus.

Though basic and simple, this prayer is for grown children as well. Have you asked Jesus into your heart? The greatest gift you can give your children is the assurance of your own eternal life. Knowing the confidence of your own salvation will bring them great peace at the time of your parting. Your confidence in God's eternal plan for your soul encourages like faith in your child. It also helps them in times of grief and sorrow when they are faced with the death of their loved ones.

It was a sad day in the life of two of my grandsons. Their PopPop went home to be with the Lord after a long illness. Both of them were comforted by their grandfather's life of service and character and by his strong faith. The hope of heaven did not override the reality of their loss. Rather, it completed it. The older one expressed the fact that things would be different without PopPop, while stating that he knew he was in heaven. He would see PopPop again, and for now it was good to know he was no longer suffering. The preschooler shared his honest feelings at PopPop's memorial service. "PopPop can't see me through that flag, you know? He can't hear me either. But it's OK. PopPop is in heaven now." How grateful I am to know firsthand that my grandchildren know in their young hearts what the psalmist knew. "Precious in the sight of the Lord is the death of his saints" (Ps. 116:15).

The joy of eternal salvation is the message of the Bible. Parents and children secure in their heavenly future bring peace to life in all its seasons. Eternal life does not begin when you die; it begins when you ask Jesus into your heart. Do not delay. Make joy complete in your earthly home. "This is the day that the LORD has made; let is rejoice and be glad in it" (Ps. 118:24).

And he took the children in his arms,
put his hands on them and blessed them.
MARK 10:16

THE LESSON

What is your response to the phrase *born again*? Are you offended when it is used to describe those who have faith in God? Do you embrace the words *born again* as a term that clarifies your relationship with God? Your answers to these questions are dependent on your understanding of Jesus' words in John 3:3, "Very truly I tell you, no one can see the kingdom of God unless he is born again."

Let's turn our attention to Nicodemus; after all, he heard Jesus' words firsthand. Nicodemus so represents human thinking. It is beyond his understanding how someone can be born a second time when he is old. Further, it is a mystery to him how one can reenter his mother's womb and be reborn (John 3:4). Jesus' response to Nicodemus reveals the biblical truth about spiritual rebirth. Our mothers gave birth to our flesh. Only Jesus can give birth to our spirit. Only through Jesus can we be born again. Jesus is God's only Son. He is our only Savior. His is the only Righteousness that covers our sin before a holy God.

ONLY SON

God identified Jesus as his Son at his baptism and when He was transfigured on the mountain in view of his disciples (Matt. 3:17, 17:5). Both times God said, "This is my Son, whom I love; with him I am well pleased." The words Jesus spoke to Nicodemus about God's only Son are the foundation of the Christian church. "For God so loved the world that he gave his one and only Son that whoever believes in him shall not perish but have eternal life" (John 3:16). When the angel spoke to Mary, the mother of Jesus, he said, "You will be with child and give birth to a son, and you are to give him the name Jesus. He will be great and be called the Son of the Most High" (Luke 1:31-32). Mary's son is God's Son, and out of God's love for the world, He sacrificed his Son so that those who believe in God's only Son will have eternal life. Nicodemus stood face to face with God's only Son!

ONLY SAVIOR

Jesus gave Nicodemus an example of salvation that he would understand—the bronze snake. As a Pharisee, Nicodemus knew about the bronze snake. In the days of Moses, when the Israelites were in the desert, they became greatly dissatisfied and spoke against Moses and God. In response to their bitter complaining, God sent deadly snakes among them. When faced with a life and death situation, the people came to Moses and said, "'We sinned when we spoke against the Lord and against you. Pray that the Lord will take the snakes away from us.' So Moses prayed for the people. The Lord said to Moses, 'Make a snake and put it up on a pole; anyone who is bitten can look at it and live'" (Num. 21:7-8). In our human condition, we are snake-bitten by sin. Without a Savior we will die in our sinful state. Our confession of sin acknowledges our need for a Savior. Jesus became as the bronze snake when he was lifted up on a cross and died for our sins. God's only Son becomes our only Savior when we are born again.

Can you hear Jesus' heart whispering to Nicodemus inside his words? "No, Nicodemus, you do not enter into your mother's womb a second time. But you must enter into my work on the cross to be born of the Spirit and have eternal life." When we are born of the flesh, we are born of our mother and father and die a natural death. When we are born of the Spirit of God, we live eternally as God's child. "Yet to all who received him, to those who believe in his name, he gave the right to become children of God—children born not of natural descent, nor human decision or a husband's will, but born of God" (John 1:12-13). God provided eternal life through his only Son. His only Son made us right with God through his death on a cross. Jesus is our only Savior.

ONLY RIGHTEOUSNESS

This night was a liberating night for Nicodemus. During all the days and nights before, he was trusting in his own ability to be right with God by keeping the Law of Moses. Keeping the Law gave Nicodemus and others like him a false sense of security. Keeping the Law had become their religion. Religion does not give us entrance into God's Kingdom. God's Kingdom is accessed by righteousness with God that is only available through his only Son and our only Savior. Righteousness with God requires a relationship with God's only Son. That relationship comes to us by faith. By faith we have righteousness that pleases God. By faith we walk in paths of righteousness as mentioned in Psalm 23. By faith we receive the gift of eternal life. New birth makes us a new creation in Christ. "Therefore, if anyone is in Christ, the new creation has come: The old has gone, the new is here!" (2 Cor. 5:17). The *old* is our first birth. The *new* is our second birth. The old was shaped by self-righteousness. The new is Christ's righteousness imputed to us by the only Righteous One. Though it was night, Nicodemus was now walking in the light of Jesus. He was right with God through Christ's righteousness!

Are you a two-birthday mom? If so, on one birthday you celebrate the day you were born on this earth, and on the second you celebrate new life in Christ when you were born into God's Kingdom. I would be the first to say that the second birth can be easily missed. You can miss being born again when you do any of the following:

- you are religious about church attendance out of a sense of duty
- you do not feel worthy of God's love
- you have unforgiveness toward another or yourself
- you are too busy to develop a relationship with God
- you do not want to yield control of your life to God
- you do not want to risk trusting in God
- you do not believe that Jesus is God's Son
- you do not believe the Bible is true
- you think that God is so loving that He will welcome everyone into heaven
- you do not think that Jesus is the only way to heaven
- you think you are a good enough person to have eternal life without a Savior
- you do not believe God could ever forgive your past

Now I will also be the first to say that if any of these "whens" are keeping you from an eternal relationship with God through his only Son, then Jesus died in vain for your sins. Listen! Listen! Listen!

- *I have loved you with an everlasting love; I have drawn you with loving-kindness.*
  JEREMIAH 31:3

- *Now this is eternal life: that they may know you, the only true God, and Jesus Christ you have sent.*
  JOHN 17:3

- *Be perfect, therefore, as your heavenly Father is perfect.*
  MATTHEW 5:48

- *. . . for all have sinned and fall short of the glory of God.*
  ROMANS 3:23

- *For the wages of sin is death, but the gift of God is eternal life in Christ Jesus, our Lord.*

ROMANS 6:23

- *For by grace you have been saved through faith—and that not from yourselves, it is the gift of God—not by works so no one can boast.*

EPHESIANS 2:8-9

- *I am the way and the truth and the life. No one comes to the Father except through me.*

JOHN 14:6

- *Salvation is found in no one else, for there is no other name under heaven by which we must be saved.*

ACTS 4:12

- *All men are like grass, and all their glory is like the flowers of the field; the grass withers and the flowers fall, but the word of the Lord stands forever.*

ISAIAH 40:6, 8

- *Here I am! I stand at the door and knock. If anyone hears my voice and opens the door, I will come in and eat with him, and he with me.*

REVELATION 3:20

- *Seek the Lord while he may be found; call on him while he is near.*

ISAIAH 55:6

- *Yes, I am coming soon.*

REVELATION 22:20

God wants to nourish your faith by satisfying the longing in your heart to be in right relationship to your heavenly Father. God is calling you to be his child either for the first time or in a deeper way. He feeds our faith through his Word. John 6:35 says, "Then Jesus declared, 'I am the bread of life. He who comes to me will never go hungry, and he who believes in me will never be thirsty.'"

Years ago the children's prayer "Now I Lay Me Down to Sleep" was often said at bedtime. "Now I lay me down to sleep. I pray the Lord my soul to keep. If I should die before I wake, I pray the Lord my soul to take." As a child, my friend was afraid to say the line "if I should die before I wake." But after she asked Jesus into her heart, she had a peace about her physical death. She knew her soul belonged to the Lord and she could trust Him with it. Personally, I had such a positive attitude that the phrase never bothered me. However, one night I realized that I was self-righteous by trusting in my good works, and I transferred my trust for eternal life to Jesus. At the time, I recall thinking that I should have been afraid to say the dying before waking line without Jesus in my heart as my only Savior. Like Nicodemus, I was living in a false sense of security. My positive thinking overrode this truth: Freedom to die in Christ gives freedom to live in Christ. "If you hold to my teaching, you are really my disciples. Then you will know the truth, and the truth will set you free" (John 8:31-32).

While in southern Spain years ago, we visited a small mountainside village on a Sunday morning. On the way up the mountain by car, I marveled at the town nestled in stone. The white houses with tile roofs and the beautiful church looked like a painting. I was determined to get a closer look. Once on foot, we meandered through the narrow streets. The sound of festive music echoed off the mountainside. All the doors of the small and tightly packed abodes were open. The elderly sat in their doorways. The lace curtains seemed to breathe with the breeze as they blew in and out of the open windows. After winding our way down the steep slope, we came to the source of the music. It was a fiesta. There was dancing and laughter in the court just outside of the church. While we were watching the celebration, my son overheard the conversation of two young men. He looked at us and said, "We're not welcome here." As we politely left the scene, I had a real sense that we were where we did not belong. We were foreign intruders at a fiesta to which we were not invited.

On my climb back up the mountainside, past all the charming homes bedecked with beautiful flowers, I thought of heaven's gate. I was struck with the joy of the people, even those in the doorways. Fiesta was in their souls. But fiesta for me that day was off limits. Jesus said to those who refuted his claim to be God's only Son, "I am the gate; whoever enters through me will be saved" (John 10:9). On our mountain descent, I marveled again—this time at the truth of the Gospel. No Jesus. No fiesta. Know Jesus. Know fiesta . . . forever!

The very best mother-child gift exchange is the assurance that both of you have eternal life. Sharing life in Christ with your child is like nothing else on earth. The great thing about our Nick's Night Job story is that Nicodemus didn't have to wait until he died to experience eternal life. Heaven on earth began for him when he met Jesus face to face. You do not have to wait either. If you have not already done so, join Nicodemus and me and be *born again . . .*

I write these things to you who believe in the name
of the Son of God so that you may know you have eternal life.
1 JOHN 5:13

THE POINT TO FAITH

I have no greater joy than to hear
that my children are walking in the truth.
3 JOHN 1:4

What brings you joy? We enjoy the accomplishments of our children. We revel in their successes. We take pleasure in every challenge met and every accolade spoken about them. But true joy only comes with a true walk with the one true God. And that walk is available only through God's Son, Jesus. That is the message of John 3:16. And that's the truth! May it be the great joy of your life to know that your children are walking in the Truth.

PRAYER: *Eternal God, I am in awe of your love for all people. Thank You for giving your Son as a means of salvation. I earnestly ask You to give me the joy of my salvation. Allow me to experience the joy of knowing that my children walk in your truth. In Jesus' Name I pray. Amen.*

PART III

Bread of Life

And Jesus said to them, "I am the bread of life. He who comes to Me shall never hunger, and he who believes in Me shall never thirst."

JOHN 6:35 NKJV

Trust in the Lord with all your heart and
lean not on your own understanding;
in all your ways acknowledge him and
he will make your paths straight.

PROVERBS 3:5-6

BOY TO MAN

THE STORY

(SEE GENESIS 37, 39-50)

It was not his fault that his father, Jacob, loved Joseph more than his brothers. Genesis 37:3 says, "Now Israel loved Joseph more than any of his other sons, because he had been born to him in his old age." For certain, it was wrong of Jacob, renamed *Israel* by God, to favor Joseph. However, his feelings toward Joseph are understandable. Joseph's mother was the love of Jacob's life. As a young man, he worked fourteen years for the right to marry Rachel and then waited many years until Joseph was born. Jacob showed his love to Joseph by making him a richly ornamented robe. Not only was it a beautiful robe, it was one that signified royalty. When he was seventeen years old, Joseph added to his brothers' ire by telling them of two dreams he'd had. He told his brothers that in one of his dreams they "were binding sheaves of grain out in the field when suddenly my sheaf rose and stood, while your sheaves gathered around mine and bowed down to it" (Gen. 37:6-7). In the other dream, Joseph said, "the sun and the moon and eleven stars were bowing down to me" (Gen. 37:9). This was all they needed to hear. In their jealousy, they threw Joseph into a pit, meaning to leave him for dead. They changed their mind, however, and sold him instead into slavery to Midianite merchants on their way to Egypt.

It was not his fault that Joseph ended up in the house of Potiphar, an Egyptian official. It was also not his fault that he was well built and handsome. These two "it was not his faults" led to a false accusation by Potiphar's wife, and Joseph landed in jail. Dreams had gotten Joseph into this mess in the first place, and as God would have it, dreams would get him out of it. He became known for interpreting dreams correctly. Each time, he gave credit to God as the one who revealed to him the meaning. Eventually, he was called to interpret the dreams of Pharaoh himself. Because Pharaoh believed what Joseph said his God would do—bring a famine to the land—Pharaoh trusted Joseph's plan for preparing for the drought and made him second in command in Egypt.

It was not Joseph's fault that there was a famine in the land that spread to his homeland. Eventually, it brought his brothers to Egypt in search of grain. Joseph's gifted handling of the seven years of plenty and the seven years of famine provided food for the land's people. And eventually, Joseph's own dreams came true. His brothers bowed down to this powerful man in Egypt. There is another "eventually." Eventually, Joseph, his brothers, and his dear father, Jacob, were reunited, and they lived together in the land of Egypt.

The circumstances of Joseph's life were beyond Joseph's understanding, but in every one of them, he trusted in the Lord God. God used what was not Joseph's fault to accomplish his plan for Israel. After Jacob died, his brothers became afraid that Joseph would hold a grudge against them and pay them back for the wrongs they'd done to him (Gen. 50:15). The boy who had become a man said to them, "Don't be afraid. Am I in the place of God? You intended to harm me, but God intended it for good to accomplish what is now being done, the saving of many lives" (Gen. 50:19-20). Indeed, the boy born to Jacob and Rachel had become a man of God for the generations.

The Nourishment

Trust in the Lord with all your heart and lean
not on your own understanding; in all your ways acknowledge
him and he will make your paths straight.

Proverbs 3:5-6

There is not another Bible character that needed the wisdom of Proverbs 3:5-6 more than Joseph. In his life he faced danger, was betrayed, forgotten, tempted, framed, and punished unjustly. If he hadn't trusted the Lord with all his heart and acknowledged God in all his ways, Joseph would have been listed as just another seed of Jacob. And what's more, the hopes of the Israelite nation would have died during the widespread famine. In his own understanding, he may have retaliated against his brothers and thwarted God's plan for his people. Rather, Joseph cooperated fully with the Father's plan. By now we know that Father knows best.

PROVERBS 3:5-6 CAN CHANGE
YOUR CHILD'S LIFE. TEACHING THEM TO SEE THINGS
THROUGH GOD'S EYES WILL YIELD IN THEM
A DETERMINATION TO TRUST GOD.

Whether you are raising a Joseph or a Josephina, Proverbs 3:5-6 can change your child's life. Teaching them to see things through God's eyes will yield in them a determination to trust God. Regularly connect their circumstances to God's overshadowing. Build in them a sense of destiny that will help them endure hardship and suffering. Give your child a process to evaluate circumstances and trust God in them. Remind them when you see the hand of God in their everyday life so they will connect God's guidance and direction in the larger events they face. Consistent referral to Proverbs 3:5-6 will foster reliance on the Lord.

Through my husband's profession I have learned to view the happenings of life through what I call The DX/RX Principle. As an internist and geriatrician, his forte is diagnosis and treatment—DX and RX. He has been trained to evaluate body systems and come to a conclusion regarding a diagnosis. With the cause of the health issue identified, Dr. Paul prescribes the appropriate treatment. We live in an age when medical information is only as far away as the Internet. There is a rush to identify our symptoms and gain understanding of how to manage our physical well-being. The best scenario, however, for physical wellness is a patient/physician relationship that is based on trust in the doctor's ability to practice his or her profession on our behalf. As our Creator, God is our ultimate Physician. He knows what ails our souls, and He knows how to bring healing. The Lord knows our DX and our RX. When we trust God with what we do not understand, we accept his diagnosis of our spiritual health. Arm your children with God's Word and teach them to trust God to work on their behalf for their physical, emotional, and spiritual health. In this way, they will learn to face life with confidence and courage. In this way, they will live in anticipation of God's goodness in their lives.

Are you in a pit or entrapped by injustice? Do you feel forgotten? Is betrayal plaguing your heart and soul? Has tragedy scarred your path? Memorize Proverbs 3:5-6. Repeat it every time your circumstances bear down on you. Be a living example of trust in God's sovereign power. It will not be wasted on your family.

You will keep in perfect peace him whose mind is
steadfast, because he trusts in you.
ISAIAH 26:3

THE LESSON

My husband's intent was to entertain and instruct the night he portrayed Joseph at our coed Bible study. Certainly he hadn't planned on being humorous. Dressed in a colorful robe (made of two tablecloths) with a headdress, bare legs, and sandals, he introduced himself as Joseph, the son of Jacob. "I was my father's favorite son," he began. "He gave me this beautiful robe." As if to show off his robe, he lifted his left arm in the air. When he did, the sleeve slipped to his elbow and exposed his wrist. There was a watch on it. "He gave me the watch, too." Just that quickly he blew his character. The watch line was not part of the script, but the truth is that if watches were available in the nineteenth century BC, Jacob would have given Joseph a Rolex. The problem was not what he gave to Joseph. The problem was what he did not give to his other sons. We might call Jacob's tents dysfunctional. He had twelve sons with four different mothers. He was passive in his discipline and partial in his favor. Ten of his sons were jealous and hated number eleven. Number twelve was protected like a prized heifer. And yet, Jacob, whom God renamed Israel, was used by God to establish the nation of Israel, the apple of God's eye. His sons became the all important heads of the twelve tribes of Israel. The lives of Jacob and his offspring are trophies of God's sovereignty and give us grounds for implementing Proverbs 3:5-6 in our lives and the lives of our children. *Faith Feedings* is all about building faith in the family, so let's examine aspects of Israel's family that are inherent to every family.

FAVORITISM

Nothing will wreck family relationships more than playing favorites. Jacob's love for Joseph and his younger brother, Benjamin, is understandable. From the time Jacob first laid eyes on Rachel, he loved her. Jacob agreed to work for Laban, Rachel's father, for seven years to earn the right to marry Rachel. When the seven years passed, however, Rachel's father gave her older and less appealing sister, Leah, to Jacob in marriage. In spite of Laban's trickery, Jacob was willing to work another seven years to have Rachel for his wife. Fourteen years did not dampen Jacob's love for Rachel. The family tent scene was pregnant with pregnancies. It took two wives and two maidservants to round out the tribe. Beloved Rachel's first child was Joseph. Her second son, Benjamin, cost Rachel her life. Yes, we can understand Jacob's extraordinary love for Rachel's sons. But, we cannot justify favoritism from a parental point of view. Jacob should have known better.

But, Jacob's own upbringing was tainted by partial parents. Father Isaac loved huntsman Esau. Mother Rebekah, on the other hand, preferred the quiet and sensitive Jacob. Favoritism in Isaac and Rebekah's camp was further compounded by the fact that Esau and Jacob were twins. Unfortunately, Jacob's family history was repeated in his generation.

Our heavenly Father showed no favorites when He sent his Son to die on a cross; He gave his life for all humankind. Do you have a child under your care that is easier to love than the others? Perhaps he or she shares your heart and soul for life. I urge you to look for what is good in the others. Ask God to make you an impartial mom. Were you a favored, or perhaps disfavored, child in your family? Ask God to intervene in your history and set you on a new path for the sake of your children and the future He has planned for them. Guard against partiality in your family. Follow the scriptural mandate as written in James 2:1: "My brothers and sisters, believers in our glorious Lord Jesus Christ must not show favoritism."

JEALOUSY AND HATRED

"When his brothers saw that their father loved him more than any of them, they hated him and could not speak a kind word to him" (Gen. 37:4). There it is in black and white, the reason and the result for all to read. Now we know why Jacob showed favoritism and why the brothers hated Joseph. But what we know is nothing more than an excuse for ungodly behavior. There is no room for jealousy or hatred in a life of faith. The black and white of God's commandments is there for all to see: "Do not covet" (Exod. 20:17) and "love one another" (John 13:34).

We are not talking about sibling rivalry here. We are talking about sibling sin. Ultimately, all sin is against God. Do you have a brother or sister who is estranged from you because of jealousy and hatred? Be quick to ask God for forgiveness. Do not postpone begging forgiveness or offering forgiveness to your sister or brother. Excuses will not do here. Tomorrow is not just another day. It is your eternity and your brother or sister's eternity as well. Do not waste it on jealousy and hatred. It is hurtful to any parent to watch strife between their children. Even more, it is hurtful to our Father in heaven. Let the words of the apostle Paul in Colossians 3:13 be your standard: "Bear with each other and forgive whatever grievances you may have against one another. Forgive as the Lord forgave you."

A PRIDEFUL ATTITUDE

Joseph is one of the most celebrated characters of the Bible. He is every mother's ideal son: honest, full of integrity, trustworthy, godly, very wise, handsome, and very successful. In addition, Joseph saved many lives and was used by God to change the history of the world. Genesis 37, however, recounts three things that Joseph did to fuel the jealousy and hatred of his brothers:

- *Joseph, a young man of seventeen, was tending flocks with his brothers . . . and he brought their father a bad report about them* (Gen. 37:2). Joseph was a tattletale. He made himself look good in his father's eyes by degrading his brothers.
- *Joseph had a dream, and when he told it to his brothers, they hated him all the more* (Gen. 37:5). Joseph's dream pictured himself being raised up and his brothers bowing down to him. They hated the thought of being under his rule.

- *"Listen," he said, "I had another dream, and this time the sun, the moon, and eleven stars were bowing down to me"* (Gen. 37:9). Even his father took offense to this dream. Would the whole family bow to Joseph?

Little did Joseph know that his future held a time of great suffering and refinement. Sometimes that is what is needed to cure us of our pride. "Pride goes before destruction, a haughty spirit before a fall" (Prov. 16:18). Joseph's prideful attitude toward his brothers landed him in a pit only to be sold as a slave.

Favoritism, hatred, jealousy, and pride represent only a slice of the human traits that are destructive to Israel's family. Joseph's life is a tribute to God's grace and faithfulness. He took a boy hated by his brothers and grew him into a man his brothers honored and respected and, yes, a man to whom his brothers eventually bowed. By faith in Joseph's God, dreams do come true.

Three Growing Robes framed Joseph's life. Each one represents a season of his life. In each season we see that he did not lean on his own understanding but acknowledged God in all his ways. Surely, the Lord did direct his path.

A RICHLY ORNAMENTED ROBE *(See Genesis 37:3)*

Jacob's robe gift to Joseph was more than a garment. Jacob gave his son a royal robe, and Joseph grew to be a royal figure in the court of the Pharaoh of Egypt. On the surface, Joseph's robe represented his father's love for Rachel's firstborn. In Jacob's heart, Joseph was his firstborn son. In giving Joseph a richly ornamented robe, Jacob exalted Joseph in the eyes of all to a regal future. As the story unfolds, Jacob's hopes were devastated when the colorful robe was returned to him bloodstained by Joseph's older brothers (Gen. 37:31-32). Jacob gave his son up for dead and grieved accordingly. The brothers had delivered the ultimate pain to a father—the loss of his precious child. But God had other plans for Jacob's favored son. At the insistence of Leah's first and fourth sons, Reuben and Judah, Joseph was spared and sold for twenty shekels of silver to the Ishmaelites. It was off to Egypt for Joseph.

What was Joseph's thinking when he was thrown into the dry cistern? In his own understanding, he was expecting death. In that cistern, Joseph learned the most important lesson of life: Look up to God. Can you picture Joseph in that deep, dark hole? If he looked down he saw nothing but himself and hopeless darkness. If he looked up he saw a small circle of light. Joseph saw a ray of hope. What was he thinking as he was carted from his homeland? The ray of hope was in his heart. The God who saved him from the pit would be with him in the foreign land. Joseph went on in hope. His brothers returned in guilt. Joseph internalized the words of Proverbs 3:5-6: "Trust in the Lord with all your heart and lean not on your own understanding; acknowledge him in all your ways and he will direct your path."

A SERVANT'S CLOAK *(See Genesis 39-41)*

In God's providence, Joseph was bought by Potiphar, the captain of the guards of the Egyptian Pharaoh at the time. This part of Joseph's life reads like a soap opera. The well-built and handsome servant became an attraction to his boss' wife. She, however, was unable to lure him into her bed. When faced with temptation, the servant ran. Unfortunately, he left his cloak in her hands. The robe of this season of Joseph's life landed him in another pit: the king's prison.

Once again, Joseph looked to the light at the end of the cistern. Once again, God was with him and placed him in positions of favor. Once again, God implemented his plan for Joseph. His past experience with dreams served him well, and Joseph became known as an interpreter of dreams. Eventually, he was called to tell Pharaoh the meaning of his disturbing dreams. Always, Joseph acknowledged God as the only one who could interpret dreams. Always, God lifted Joseph up. At the end of the day, he became second to Pharaoh. Joseph had gone from pit to prison to palace. The words of Proverbs were Joseph's reality: "Trust in the Lord with all your heart and lean not on your own understanding; acknowledge him in all your ways and he will direct your path."

A ROBE OF FINE LINEN, A GOLD CHAIN, AND THE KING'S SIGNET RING
(See Genesis 41:41-43)

Add to this a chariot and all authority over Egypt, and you have a man at the top of his game. That man, Joseph, had grown fully into his father's robe of many colors. Joseph was right where God wanted him. The Bible records the rest of the story. Joseph stored grain in plenty and sold grain in want. He saved the people of Egypt from death by famine and gained all their property for Pharaoh. In the meantime, he was miraculously reunited with his family. In the end, dear Jacob died in his favored son's arms. Most importantly, the Lord made his people a nation through Rachel's pride and joy. Joseph's life signified the words of the future and greatest king of Israel, King David. "The Lord will fulfill his purpose for me; your love, O Lord, endures forever" (Ps. 138:8). Once more I say, "Trust in the Lord with all your heart and lean not on your own understanding; acknowledge him in all your ways and he will direct your path."

I know a young woman who learned the principle of this verse through her own "cistern" experience. Sue had a plan for her life. She would graduate from college, get married, work at her profession, save money for a permanent home, and begin a family. Sue was well into living out her hopes and dreams when her plan met with an intruder. In the ensuing months, Sue learned that her plan was a good plan, but it was not God's plan.

Sue and her new husband loved the location of their new home. It was close to their respective workplaces. Their unobstructed view of the woods and open area gave the newlyweds a sense of privacy. It was an ideal first home in every way, and they quickly settled into a routine. Each day after a quick breakfast, Sue and her husband parted with a hug and a kiss. He always left first, and she followed ten minutes later. Sue found security in living out her plans. It was so . . . ideal.

On a frigid day in January, ideal was interrupted. Hubby left their abode on schedule. Sue tidied up the kitchen, dressed in her heavy winter coat and gloves, and gathered her workday supplies. With a plan to dart through the cold to her car, she opened her secluded front door. At that very moment, Sue found her security compromised. Looming in the doorway was a man wearing a mask and carrying a Taser. Thank God for the heavy winter coat she was wearing. And by all means, thank God that she warded off her attacker, who fled into the woods from which he had come.

Many years later, in the midst of a beautiful family life, Sue knows that day of personal terror was a turning point in her life. The way was not easy and not as she had planned, but eventually God redeemed her spoiled plans. In God's plan, a home became available in the neighborhood where Sue grew up. The sellers took the first offer on the home, even though it was below the asking price. In the healing process, Sue gained a new sense of security in God's grace and mercy. As her faith grew, she learned that she didn't have to control everything or anything, for that matter. She learned the premise of Proverbs 3:5-6. With several years between the present and that January morning, Sue acknowledges God daily and trusts his plan and purpose for her life. It is her priority to teach her children that God's plan is the best plan. Sue's new normal is based on a heavenly ideal, and she is thriving in it.

Pattern your Growing Robe for your child after the character of Joseph. In every season of his life, Joseph acknowledged God and God acknowledged Joseph. Thousands of years later, another favored Son was born. His first robe was a humble swaddling cloth in a manger. Later, he, too, wore the clothes of a servant. Now he wears the robe of the King of Kings. This is what He said about acknowledging God in your life: "Whoever acknowledges me before men, I will acknowledge him before my Father in heaven" (Matt. 10:32). Therein we have the essence of the eleventh son of Israel.

Turn to me and be saved, all you ends of the earth;
for I am God and there is no other.
ISAIAH 45:22

THE POINT TO FAITH

Trust in the Lord with all your heart and
lean not on your own understanding; acknowledge him
and he will make your paths straight.
PROVERBS 3:5-6

The challenge of the Christian life is to forsake our own understanding for the sake of trusting God with our day-to-day and our destiny. As we grow, however, in the knowledge of the person of God through the Bible and the faithfulness of God through answered prayer, our trust shifts. Acknowledge God's wisdom and power as his Holy Spirit reveals it to you. Get ready. Straight paths ahead!

PRAYER: *Eternal God, I pray that You will allow me to view life through your eyes. Help me to give my children hope to carry on and the character to endure. May we as a family acknowledge You in all our ways as we seek to follow your way for our lives. In Jesus' Name I pray. Amen.*

FAITH FEEDING 10

"For I know the plans I have for you,"
declares the Lord, "plans to prosper you and not to harm you,
plans to give you hope and a future."

JEREMIAH 29:11

EXILED FAITH

THE STORY

(SEE DANIEL 1)

Certainly, it wasn't the plan Daniel's parents had for their son. On the other hand, they knew it was a possibility. Judah's sin against God was great. Surely God would not contend with them forever. Earthly "forever" had come. Of the twenty reigning kings in Jerusalem, only eight of them "did what was right in the eyes of the Lord." About the other twelve, the Bible says they "did evil in the eyes of the Lord" (1& 2 Kings, 1 & 2 Chronicles). Their evil was complete. They worshipped carved wood and poured metal that could do nothing for them. They scorned, denied, and rejected the Living God who could do everything for them. They sacrificed their children to a man-made god called Molech and tainted their sacrifices to a God who is holy. Indeed, the earthly kingdom of Judah was in jeopardy. As believers in the one true God and as people who "did what was right in the eyes of the Lord," Daniel's family had become foreigners in their own country. They thanked God for the eight kings who followed the ways of the Lord. Through them, God saved a remnant for Himself.

Daniel shared the faith of his parents. He was "trained in the way he should go" and as a young man "he would not depart from it" (Prov. 22:6). Never, he vowed, would he turn away from the God who had brought Father Abraham from beyond the River. His family embraced the words of their ancestor, Joshua: "But as for me and my household, we will serve the Lord" (Josh. 24:15). Daniel's life bore witness to his vow to the Lord. He took his faith with him into exile—even into the enemy territory called Babylon. He was without parents or siblings or familiar environment. But he was not without his God.

Daniel was chosen by God and by the king of Babylon. He fit King Nebuchadnezzar's job description: "Bring in some of the Israelites from the royal family and nobility—young men without any physical defect, handsome, showing aptitude for every kind of learning, well informed, quick to understand, and qualified to serve in the king's palace" (Dan. 1:3-4). His faith in God was the one qualification not important to the earthly king. However, it was the most important to the heavenly King. God would use the faith of Daniel and his three friends to demonstrate his mighty power to the conqueror of his people.

Daniel, renamed Belteshazzar, and his three cohorts, Shadrach, Meshach, and Abednego, were fed like kings and trained like scholars. They learned languages and sciences. God honored their refusal to defile themselves with royal food by causing the official in charge to "show favor and sympathy." And God Himself was their teacher. "To these four men God gave knowledge and understanding of all kinds of literature and learning. And Daniel could understand visions and dreams" (Dan. 1:17). When the time came for their interview with the king, he "found none equal to them . . . In every matter of wisdom and understanding about which the king questioned them, he found them ten times better that all the magicians and enchanters in his whole kingdom" (Dan. 1:19-20). God always equips the called of God for the call of God. Daniel was ready for the task at hand.

Daniel remained faithful to God in exile, and God showed his faithfulness to Daniel and his friends. His friends came out of a fire pit alive, and Daniel survived a den of lions. They were exalted in the kingdom of Babylon while they worked for the kingdom of God. No dream was too hard for Daniel to interpret. No prophecy failed. No challenge was too great. No work was left undone. Through Daniel, God revealed his plans for the end of Babylon and the end of time.

God's plan for Israel's exile was seventy years. In every one of those years, Daniel served God. Daniel's testimony about God was sure and full of truth. Daniel was a Joseph in his time. Like Joseph, Daniel knew the secret of exiled faith: God goes with you in it.

Then Daniel praised God and said, "Praise be
to the name of God forever and ever; wisdom and power are his.
He changes times and seasons;
he sets up kings and deposes them. He gives wisdom
to the wise and knowledge
to the discerning. He reveals deep and hidden things;
he knows what lies in darkness, and light dwells with him."
DANIEL 2:18-22

THE NOURISHMENT

"For I know the plans I have for you,"
declares the Lord, "plans to prosper you and not to harm you,
plans to give you hope and a future."
JEREMIAH 29:11

Daniel's faith parents taught him to walk with God in the present and trust God with the future. You can imagine the trauma that Daniel experienced when he was ripped from his family and sent into captivity. And yet, the Bible says that Daniel's faith did not waiver in Babylon. Instead, he prospered in his faith and resisted being dissuaded from it. At great risk, he did not compromise his relationship with God. With confidence, he refused to bow down to anyone or anything other than God; with conviction, he refused to alter his prayer regimen; with great courage, he pronounced God's judgment against King Nebuchadnezzar and King Belshazzar. God had a specific plan for Daniel's life, and Daniel cooperated with it. The very people who were the enemy of the Jews promoted Daniel and his friends to high positions of authority.

WRITE JEREMIAH 29:11 ON A CARD
AND PUT IT ON THEIR MIRROR OR THEIR DESK.
USE IT IN THEIR NIGHTTIME PRAYERS.

The application of scriptural principles is gender free. Your Daniel and your Danielle need to live in the faith confidence, conviction, and courage of Belteshazzar, Shadrach, Meshach, and Abednego. Read them the stories of the Bible so that they can know the outcome of trusting God. Refer often to God's eternal plan so that they will have hope in his present plan. Teach them how to walk by faith so that they live in cooperation with God's plan in the present. Write Jeremiah 29:11 on a card and put it on their mirror or their desk. Use it in their nighttime prayers. And by all means, speak with words of hope in God and show them by your faith that you know that God knows the plans for their mother as well.

Then you will call upon me and come and pray to me,
and I will listen to you.
You will seek me and find me when
you seek me with all your heart.
JEREMIAH 29:12-13

THE LESSON

In the Old Testament accounts of the Bible, God spoke to people either directly, through dreams, or through prophets. Jeremiah was a prophet that spoke the word of the Lord to God's people during the period of the kings of Israel. Jeremiah did not work alone. There were many prophets who spoke the message of God, but there was only one message. Repeatedly the prophets exhorted the kings, the priests, the leaders, and the people to repent of their sins and return to God. God always desires to extend grace, mercy, and forgiveness. The message of the prophets was as a Father calling his children back into right relationship. The prophet Joel expressed it with the term *rend your heart*. "'Even now,' declares the Lord, 'return to me with all your heart . . . rend your heart, and not your garments. Return to the Lord your God, for he is gracious and compassionate, slow to anger and abounding in love'" (Joel 2:12-13).

The fact that our story related Daniel's exiled faith tells us that the people did not receive or obey the message of God through the prophets. In fact, in many cases they harmed, persecuted, and even killed the prophets. Repenting of their sin against God, returning to an obedient relationship with God, and rending their hearts toward God proved to be a sacrifice the people refused. In the year 586 BC, the day of the Lord arrived, and Judah fell to the Chaldeans. Listen to the words of 2 Chronicles 36:20-21: "[King Nebuchadnezzar] carried into exile to Babylon the remnant, who escaped the sword, and they became servants to him and his sons until the kingdom of Persia came into power. The land enjoyed its sabbath rests; all the time of its desolation it rested, until the seventy years were completed in fulfillment of the word of the Lord spoken by Jeremiah."

It is this context—the Babylonian exile—that we find our Faith Feeding principle from Jeremiah 29:11. God was speaking to the remnant of faith believers about their life away from their homeland. Through Jeremiah (29:4-14), God told them the plan for the next seventy years:

> This is what the Lord Almighty, the God of Israel, says to all
> I carried into exile from Jerusalem to Babylon:
> "Build houses and settle down; plant gardens and eat what
> they produce. Marry and have sons and daughters;
> find wives for your sons and give your daughters in marriage,
> so that they too may have sons and daughters. Increase
> in number there; do not decrease. Also, seek peace and prosperity
> of the city to which I have carried you into exile. Pray to the Lord for it,
> because if it prospers, you too will prosper." Yes, this is what
> the God of Israel says: "Do not let the prophets and diviners among
> you deceive you. Do not listen to the dreams you encourage
> them to have. They are prophesying lies to you in my name.
> I have not sent them," declares the Lord. This is what the Lord says:
> "When seventy years are completed for you in Babylon, I will come
> to you and fulfill my gracious promise to bring you back to this place.
> For I know the plans I have for you," declares the Lord, "plans
> to prosper you and not to harm you, plans to give you a hope and a
> future. Then you will call upon me and come and pray to me,
> and I will listen to you. You will seek me and find me when you seek me
> with all your heart. I will be found by you," declares the Lord,
> "and will bring you back from captivity. I will gather you from all the
> nations and places where I have banished you," declares the Lord, "and
> will bring you back to the place from which I carried you into exile."

Sounds like a plan to me. Just imagine, the God of the universe busied Himself with the daily life plans of a small band of people scattered in a foreign land. They must have mattered to God. Also, it mattered to God how they lived. His directions were deeply practical: Build houses, produce your own food, build families of like mind, increase in number, seek peace and prosperity, pray for the country in which you live, do not be deceived by the religion of the people. When I read this plan from God for his people, I think of Genesis 1 and 2. I picture an environment that fosters life, gardens, marriage, and family. Indeed, God has a plan for your life and mine. It matters to God how we live. Mostly, it matters to God that He matters to us. Knowing that you matter to God produces eternal hope in your heart.

Jeremiah wrote a letter of hope from God to his own people. He gave them hope to carry on in faith. In time, the Israelites would return to their land. God would move the heart of King Cyrus to release them and even have built in Jerusalem a temple of the Lord to replace the one that had been destroyed by King Nebuchadnezzar. God knew the plans for them. In faith, they knew they could trust God. Trust in God breeds hope for living a life of faith in good times and in hard times.

On the Easter Sunday prior to this writing, I flew home after visiting with my children and their families. My plane connection time was much shorter than I like and required racing through the Atlanta airport. My seat, 27C, was assigned, literally, as I walked into the jet way. Being the last on the plane, I navigated past a sold-out passenger list to the back of the plane. There was a young man in 27C. He appeared to be sleeping. I gently tapped him on the shoulder and offered to sit in 27B—the only remaining seat on the plane. He smiled and moved over one seat. Once settled into 27C, I pulled out my Bible study lesson to complete, and he settled in to complete his nap. I have high regard for where God seats me on a plane, and I prayed that I could say something kind and encouraging to 27B. After awhile, he switched his position and cupped his hands to hold his head. I noticed that his tattoos were not limited to his arms. On this young man's hand I saw letters. H on the pointer finger, O on "tall man," and P on his ring finger. I could not see "pinky," but I naturally assumed it bore an E. As we prepared for landing, he woke up from his nap, and I tried to land a conversation. We chatted about where he had been and where he lived. The wheels were lowered. *Time is short!* I thought. With great sincerity I said, "I am fascinated by your tattoos. I have never seen tattoos that were only black with no color. And I couldn't help but notice the letters on your right hand. I couldn't see your little finger but my guess is that is has an E on it to spell hope."

"Oh no," 27B said as he crossed his hands and held them out for me to see. My eyes landed on the letters of his right and left hand just as he said, "Both hands go together to spell *Hopeless.*"

Well, this caught 27C by surprise but did not render her speechless! Within the blink of an eye I said, "Oh, no, you are not hopeless! I want you to sit on your left hand for the rest of your life!" The rest went something like this: Chuckle, chuckle, touchdown! Deplaning takes awhile on a full flight. This time I was glad for it. I prayed silently for this man while he was still in my presence. Then I leaned over and said, "I pray that God gives you so much hope that you do not know what to do with it all."

He responded with a smile, "Thank you, ma'am, and you have a happy Easter." Easter hope—exactly what 27B needs.

As I left the plane to face the responsibilities of home, I became heavy with a burden for the hopeless. What was this young man thinking and feeling when he had those letters etched on his skin? I wondered. The answer came swiftly. He was thinking that his life was unworthy of God's plan; that no one really cared for his well-being; that prosperity, a hope, and a future do not have his name on them. He was thinking that he does not matter to God or to anyone else.

Let me share something about 27B. That young man is representative of a growing number of young people, both boys and girls, in our midst who do not believe that they matter to God or anyone else. They are living in varying degrees of hopelessness. Now let me share something about 27C. That older woman is called to live according to the Book on her lap in such a way as to influence the hopeless to hope. In all the plans that God has for you, mother of influence, He intends for you to be a giver of hope; not hope as the world gives, as in good wishes, but hope as only God can deliver, as in meaning and purpose.

The message of the prophets was twofold; it was a message about life on earth and life in heaven. The prophecies of the men of God to Israel in the hundreds of years leading up to the fall of the northern and southern kingdoms were fulfilled to the letter. If their message is trustworthy in the temporal on earth, can we not trust them to be trustworthy in the permanence of heaven?

God's plan is for God's people to live according to God's plan. It is the pathway of blessing. It is the avenue to hope. Ultimately, God's plan goes beyond our temporary living on this earth to eternal living in heaven. At present, we are as exiles in a foreign land. At that time, we will have arrived at our place of citizenship, our homeland. Our exiled faith will prove itself trustworthy and complete. Seventy years after their exile from their homeland, the Jews returned to Judah, and the temple was rebuilt. Their faith was rightly placed in the one true God.

Just before Jesus' death, He spoke words of comfort to his disciples. "Do not let your hearts be troubled. You believe in God; believe also in me. My Father's house has many rooms; if that were not so, would I have told you that I am going there to prepare a place for you? And if I go and prepare a place for you, I will come back and take you to be with me that you also may be where I am. You know the way to the place where I am going" (John 14:1-4). Now there is a plan with a hope and a future. Believe in it. Cooperate with it. Teach your children to rely on it. Pray for them to be Daniels in their own generation.

Hear, O Israel: The Lord our God, the Lord is one.
Love the Lord your God with all your heart and
with all your soul and with all your strength.
These commandments that I give you today are
to be upon your hearts. Impress them on your children.
Talk about them when you sit at home and when you walk along
the road, when you lie down and when you get up.
Deuteronomy 6:4-7

THE POINT TO FAITH

"For I know the plans I have for you,"
declares the Lord, "plans to prosper you and not to harm you,
plans to give you hope and a future."
JEREMIAH 29:11

The concerns that plague our daily life contradict this verse. The remedy for such contradiction is found in our deepening relationship with Jesus. As we trust in the Lord, we see life from an eternal perspective. To the degree we know the love and character of God, we will trust ourselves to his plan and cooperate with it. He alone is our prosperity, our hope, and our future. That truth will dim the concerns of any day!

PRAYER: *God of Hope, I ask You to give to me a faith that is anchored in You. Impart your plan for my future to me and to my offspring. Above all things, may my children never lose hope in You. Preserve and protect them as they encounter those things that would erode in their minds the reason for their being. In Jesus' Name I pray. Amen.*

FAITH FEEDING 11

*Love the Lord your God with all your heart
and with all your soul and with all your mind.
This is the first and greatest commandment. And the second
is like it: Love your neighbor as yourself.*

MATTHEW 22:37-39

FOR GOODNESS' SAKE

THE STORY *(as told by the Good Samaritan)*

(SEE LUKE 10:25-37)

I vividly recall a trip I once took on the road between Jerusalem and Jericho. In my day, most travel was by donkey. Sometimes I walked with my animal behind me; sometimes I rode. Though not so comfortable and very dusty, traveling by foot and donkey gave me time to think about life and what was important. Little did I know that on this day my life's principles would be put to the test. From a distance I saw something on the side of the road. As I approached, I wondered, "Is it an animal or perhaps a cloak or a cart of goods?" The closer I got, the more it looked like the form of a man lying still, so I tried to move my donkey along. Was he dead? Was he injured? No, it couldn't be. Two men going the other way had already passed me. If someone were in need they surely would have told me. I heard myself say, "Oh, my Lord," at the realization that my fears were confirmed. It was a man. He looked badly beaten. My animal was too slow.

I slid off of him and pulled him behind me as fast as he would go. When I got close to the man, I began to run to him, wondering how I could help him. Was I too late?

When I reached him, I was overwhelmed with pity. Surely this man had been robbed and left for dead. As I leaned over him, I could hear him gasping for breath. Taking a moment to calm my racing heart, I opened my sack and removed a clean robe I was carrying. I ripped it into strips and bandaged his wounds. I was glad for the oil and wine I had with me. I poured it on to clean and soothe his wounds. *Who would have done such a thing?* I thought. It seemed like I had the strength of Samson as I picked this fellow up and placed him on my donkey. The road was familiar to me, and I knew of an inn nearby. We moved quickly.

Once at the inn, I washed his wounds and fed him some water and bread. He took very little, but I could see that he would survive. The next morning I gave the innkeeper two denarii and asked him to care for my new friend. I would stop on my way back. "If there is any extra expense," I told the innkeeper, "I will reimburse you on my return."

When I was on my way again, I began to recount everything that had happened. Suddenly, I remembered those two fellows who had passed me on the road. Did they pass by this man who fell into the hands of robbers and do nothing? How could that be? One had the clothes of a priest. The other looked like a Levite. "For goodness' sake," I mumbled, "I am just an ordinary Samaritan. What I did was nothing special. It was the right and just thing to do."

Years later I heard that the fellow called Jesus told my story. He wanted those Law people to understand the importance of showing mercy to others. That would be just like Jesus to speak about mercy. Mercy was important to him. I understand. Mercy is important to me as well. Jesus said that I did a good thing that day. He called me a Good Samaritan. Nah, I just did what my mother had taught me. I treated the helpless stranger on the side of the road as though he was my neighbor.

THE NOURISHMENT

Love the Lord your God with all your heart
and with all your soul and with all your mind.
This is the first and the greatest commandment.
And the second is like it: Love your neighbor as yourself.
MATTHEW 22:37-39

Three of the Gospel writers quote these two commands as the greatest in God's eyes. What is great in God's eyes should be our priority for our children. We have talked about the greatest command, "Love the Lord your God with all your heart and with all your soul and with all your mind." As we consider the second greatest commandment—"Love your neighbor as yourself"—we will see that they are uniquely related. In fact, one cannot be obeyed without the other. If we love God, we must love others. To love others according to Jesus' command, we must love God.

This Faith Feeding principle relays the greatest and the second greatest commandments. It involves teaching your child to respond to God's love for them as demonstrated by the giving of his Son. They must also learn that loving God is not complete without loving others for whom God gave his Son. In the Luke passage, Jesus illustrated love your neighbor as yourself with the parable of the Good Samaritan. He used the concept of showing mercy. Mainly you want to make your children aware of the needs of others.

ENCOURAGE THEM TO REACH OUT TO THOSE WHO ARE DIFFERENT. TEACH THEM TO PRAY FOR "THEIR NEIGHBOR."

Build an attitude of mercy. Mercy springs from a humble heart. Teach them not to be quick to judge. Encourage them to reach out to those who are different. Teach them to pray for "their neighbor." Have them ask God how they can show mercy to those God brings in their path.

It is worth noting that the love for our neighbor is sacrificial. It is like giving Jesus to others. Though kindness is involved in mercy, we must remember that kindness in itself is not the second commandment. The love of God for the heart of your neighbor must come from the love of God in your own heart. Number one and number two commandments cannot be fulfilled otherwise. Marry these commandments in the lives of your children and watch the love of God pour from their being. When you see your child showing mercy to others, be like one of my friends, Ed, and say, "You have made God smile today."

> *The King will reply, "I tell you the truth,*
> *whatever you did for one of the least of these brothers*
> *of mine, you did for me."*
> MATTHEW 25:40

THE LESSON

From the time Jesus began his public ministry at about thirty years old, he created a stir. He began by teaching in the local synagogues in the towns near his home. Each synagogue was like a classroom where he opened the Scriptures to his people, the Jews. They were amazed at the authority of his teaching. As the popularity of Jesus grew, so did his classroom. He met people in homes, fields, and walking paths. Their amazement went beyond his teaching to the power of his authority over diseases, nature, infirmities, and demons. He further grabbed their attention because of his compassion for the weak and the poor. In every synagogue and town, they expressed their awe at Jesus' understanding of the Law and his power to forgive. The people were hungry in their souls for the likes of Jesus. They responded to Him in crowds and long lines of the sick and needy.

Jesus' ministry also got the attention of the religious leaders of the day. They were threatened by his popularity and the miracles He performed. It did not take them long to try to undermine his mission. They were especially agitated by his claim to be the Son of God. At every village stop, they were there to test Him. Luke 10:25-30 describes one of the many encounters Jesus had with the experts in the Law of Moses:

> On one occasion an expert in the law stood up to test Jesus. "Teacher," he asked, "what must I do to inherit eternal life?"
>
> "What is written in the Law?" he replied. "How do you read it?"
>
> He answered: "Love the Lord your God with all your heart and with all your soul and with all your strength and with all your mind; and, love your neighbor as yourself."
>
> "You have answered correctly," Jesus replied. "Do this and you will live."
>
> But he wanted to justify himself, so he asked Jesus, "And who is my neighbor?"

In reply to the lawyer's pointed question, Jesus gave a poignant answer. He told the man and all who were listening the parable of the Good Samaritan. Parables are fictional stories with a point and a punch line. They contain examples that illustrate their meaning. The understanding of parables is hidden to some. To those who are spiritually perceptive, parables as Jesus used them teach powerful scriptural principles. Jesus took special care to make sure his disciples understood the hidden meaning of his parables. He would be with them only a short time, and their knowledge of Jesus' identity and work was essential to their faith. The parable of the Good Samaritan sent a powerful message to all who heard it.

THE TEACHERS OF THE LAW

Sadly, the teachers of the Law could identify with the priest and the Levite who passed the injured man on the other side of the road. They saw the man with their eyes, but they did not see the man as God saw him. They were not moved to show mercy toward him. Their faith was in the Law. The religious officials and teachers of the Law were blind to the heart of Jesus. Their spiritual blindness pushed them to the other side of the road. In God's eyes, the priest and the Levite were unloving, unmerciful, and unjust. Even worse, they should have known better. And far worse again, they thought they did know better. Their faith was in their knowledge and their standing. Pride had hardened their hearts.

Do you remember what Jesus said about the children? "Therefore whoever humbles himself as this little child is the greatest in the kingdom of heaven" (Matt. 18:4 NKJV). Jesus exposed the hearts of the priest and the Levite and lifted up the heart of the Samaritan. With Jesus, it is always about the heart. Jesus' standards are far different than the standards of our society. Education, training, and degrees are good, but not at the cost of a humble heart for God. As a faith mother, teach your child the priorities of a faith life: Love God, love your neighbor. Such teaching from a woman of godly influence will keep them from being pushed to the other side of the road.

THE CROWDS

Many people touched by Jesus believed and committed themselves to his teaching. Some believed but found the cost and risk of following Jesus too great. Others openly denied Jesus' message. Still others were complacent. They said they believed but bore no fruit. Many years later in his Revelation to John, Jesus would speak of the church at Laodicea: "I know your deeds, that you are neither cold nor hot. I wish you were either one or the other! So, because you are lukewarm—neither hot nor cold—I am about to spit you out of my mouth'" (Rev. 3:15-16). Wow! The one thing I do not want to be is lukewarm! When Jesus looks at crowds, he sees individual hearts. He is able to discern the faith, or the lack of it, of each one.

He told the parable of the sower in Luke 8:5-15, which compared the Word of God to a seed. In this parable, he is the farmer who scattered the seed. The soil represents the hearts of the people. The seed that fell on the rocks withered. The seed that fell on the path got trampled. The seed that fell among the thorns grew but got choked out by the weeds. But the seed that fell on good soil produced a crop. The parable of the sower would have been very meaningful to the many farmers in the crowd. Often Jesus said, "He who has ears let him hear." He spoke to the crowd at large, but his message was to those who had the heart to hear so that they would have the faith to believe.

Crowds have not changed in regard to Jesus. Good soil seems to be a rare commodity. Be sure to water and feed the soil of your child's heart so that the Word of God will take root. Be a gardener in their lives: Transplant, fertilize, weed, and pray. When I look at a crowd, I often wonder how many would be good soil for Jesus' Word if only they had a farmer to sow the seed and work the soil. Mothers are "the farmers" of children. You may be the farmer for your child's friend or your neighbor's children, too. Farmer's hours are long and arduous. In Jesus, however, you will not labor in vain. Be farmers then, for goodness' sake!

THE DISCIPLES

Jesus' chosen disciples were coming to believe every word that Jesus spoke. They'd tasted the water He changed into wine. They were in the boat for the great catch of fish. Their fears were removed when He calmed the storm. They'd passed out the food that came from five loaves and fishes and fed a multitude. They'd witnessed the leper's spotless skin, the paralytic's steps, the blind man's sight. They'd seen the demons shriek at the sight of Him. They'd heard the parables and the claims. They were of good soil, and they believed that Jesus was who He claimed to be, the Messiah. It is true that they did not understand it all, but they were sold out for their Teacher. Little did they know the test of their faith that was on the horizon. But they trusted Jesus for their eternal life.

When our children see God as the source of all that is good, their faith in God, who is only good, grows. Open their ears and eyes to what God is doing around them. We must pray that our children's faith and our own goes beyond our understanding. Deciding to follow Jesus is not enough. Becoming like Jesus is required.

The message of the Good Samaritan hit the teachers of the Law, the crowd, and the disciples right between the eyes. Calling a Samaritan good was beyond their comprehension. They had hated the Samaritans since the days of the fall of Israel. They thought them to be half-breeds not worthy of the kingdom of God. Who was this man that He called himself the Son of God and a Samaritan good? Who was this man who ate with tax collectors and sinners and broke the laws of the Sabbath? Whoever He was, He was to be feared, revered, believed, or rejected. "Jesus Christ is the same yesterday and today and forever" (Heb. 13:8). She who has ears let her hear!

We do not know the Good Samaritan's name, but we know his fame as one who showed mercy on the victim of violence. Heaven knows there are victims aplenty around us. You may not even have to go across town to find one. Just walk across the street and let mercy flow out of your heart for God and for your neighbor. As Jesus told the expert in the Law, "Go and do likewise" (Luke 10:37).

This is my command: Love each other.
JOHN 15:17

THE POINT TO FAITH

Love the Lord your God with all your heart and
with all your soul and with all your mind.

This is the first and greatest commandment.
And the second is like it: Love your neighbor as yourself.
MATTHEW 22:37-39

Jesus calls these commandments the greatest two commandments. I call them impossible. Everywhere I look, I see distractions to loving God and reasons not to love my neighbor. Such distractions and reasons surround you as well. In growing faith, we have come to understand that Jesus is the one who empowers us and enables us to love God and our neighbor. Make it your daily prayer that God will fill you with the Holy Spirit so that you can be obedient to number one and number two. It will not happen any other way.

PRAYER: *Lord God, I do pray that You will empower and enable me and those under my care to be obedient to the commandments You called the greatest. For the love of God and for the sake of goodness, fill us as a family with your Holy Spirit. In Jesus' Name I pray. Amen.*

FAITH FEEDING 12

A wife of noble character who can find?
She is worth far more than rubies.

PROVERBS 31:10

He has showed you, O man, what is good.
And what does the Lord require of you? To act justly and
to have mercy and to walk humbly with your God.

MICAH 6:8

WHEREVER YOU GO

THE STORY

(SEE BOOK OF RUTH)

Famines are family movers. Certainly that was the case in the time of the judges of Israel. The famine in Bethlehem in Judah brought husband and father Elimelech to a fork in the road. Should he stay in his homeland and risk his family to the ravages of long-term hunger or sojourn in a foreign land where the rains watered the land and the crops were abundant? Responsibility for his family loomed heavy on this Jewish dad, and on one very hot and dry day he said to his wife and boys, "Load up, we're going to Moab." Such a "fork in the road" decision was not easy for Elimelech. He was from the tribe of Ephraim and had a deep loyalty to his people. His roots were in Judah. His wife, Naomi, and his boys, Mahlon and Killion, were happy there. In a true sense, they belonged in Bethlehem. But, "for such a time as this" (Esther 4:14), the wheat and barley fields of Moab were calling their names. Whether driven by hunger or driven by destiny, Elimelech, Naomi, Mahlon, and Killion relocated in a gentile land.

Mother Naomi had no idea on the dusty road to Moab what lay ahead. All she knew was the pain of parting with a humble home, her extended family, and her lifelong friends. What Naomi didn't know was that the next decade would yield pain and grief in her life that would approach unbearable. In her own words ten years later, "Don't call me Naomi... call me Mara because the Almighty has made my life very bitter. I went away full, but the Lord has brought me back empty. Why call me Naomi?" (Ruth 1:20-21). The soil of Moab would yield food for the family of Naomi, whose name means pleasant. The society of Moab would provide wives for her two boys. But the land of Moab would become the burial ground for the beloved husband and sons of Mara, which means bitter. Empty, indeed.

Hunger for food took Naomi out of Bethlehem; hunger for home would return her. The famine ended, and the time came for Naomi to return home. She was gripped with grief at the thought of leaving her departed loved ones and her daughters-in-law. After all, they were her only connection to her boys. They were the only ones who really understood her emptiness. The girls, Orpah and Ruth, were saddened for this change point in their lives as well. Their hopes and dreams for a family had been dashed. In a scene likened to *Gone With the Wind*, Naomi released the wives of her sons to return to their homeland. "Go back, each of you, to your mother's home. May the Lord show you kindness, as you have shown kindness to your dead husbands and to me. May the Lord grant that each of you will find rest in the home of another husband" (Ruth 1:8-9). Elimelech had been blessed when young Naomi was chosen for his bride. In the midst of sorrow and sadness, his widow proved to be a mother-in-law extraordinaire. Knowing their need for husbands and families of their own, she put the welfare of her daughters-in-law above her own.

The plea to "go back" presented a fork in the road to Orpah and Ruth. In God's providence, Orpah "kissed her mother-in-law goodbye, but Ruth clung to her" (Ruth 1:14). One returned to her own land, her own people, and her own gods. The other chose a new identity: Naomi's land, Naomi's people, Naomi's God. Ruth's words are among the most beautiful in all of Scripture. They signify the deepest and most God-honoring relationship possible between a woman and the mother of her husband. "But Ruth replied, 'Don't urge me to leave you or turn back from you. Where you go I will go, and where you stay I will stay. Your people will be my people and your God will be my God. Where you die I will die, and there I will be buried. May the Lord deal with me ever so severely, if even death separates you and me" (Ruth 1:16-17). With the words, "where you go I will go," Ruth, the Moabitess, made a fork-in-the-road decision that would set her destiny and yours and mine as well.

As Bethlehem would later be prepared for the Christ Child, Bethlehem was prepared for Ruth. The pair arrived in Bethlehem as the barley harvest was beginning (Ruth 1:22). The season was set for Ruth to provide food for Naomi and herself. She would glean the fields after the harvesters, as such was the Jewish custom of providing for the poor. In God's perfect timing and plan, Ruth found favor in the fields of Boaz. Boaz, a man of great godly character and integrity, heard of Ruth's kindness toward Naomi. "I have been told all about what you have done for your mother-in-law since the death of your husband—how you left your father and mother and your homeland and came to live with a people you did not know before" (Ruth 2:11). Ruth's compassion for Naomi registered in the heart of Boaz. In response, he made provisions for Ruth to glean the fields in safety. He offered her nourishment at mealtime and food to gather to take home to Naomi. As Ruth was following after the servant girls gleaning the grain that they missed, she must have sighed in relief and joy. In her heart she had wondered if Naomi's people would accept her and whether or not she would be able to provide for her mother-in-law. Ruth's heart of compassion and service met with Boaz's kindness and generosity. Surely her resolve said, "Your land, your people, your God. Everything is going to be okay."

While Ruth was gleaning day after day, Naomi was doing what mothers-in-law do best: planning. Healing had come to Naomi, and the future, rather than the past, began to fill her thoughts. She knew well the Jewish provision for a Kinsman-Redeemer. In order to continue the line and family name of the dead, a kinsman could buy the land and marry the widow. Boaz was a kinsman from the clan of Elimelech. In Naomi's eyes, he had shown himself worthy of Ruth. It was time to move from the fields of harvest to the threshing floor. Naomi gave Ruth a 101 course on how to offer herself as a bride to a kinsman. Ruth was a quick study. She was also totally committed to Naomi. They were now as daughter and mother. Ruth's willingness to follow Naomi's instructions was born out of trust of Naomi and her God. Without hesitation, Ruth readied herself by following Naomi's instructions: "Wash, put on perfume and get dressed in your best clothes" (Ruth 3:3).

Can you imagine what was going through Ruth's mind as she approached the threshing floor? She may even have thought, *I'd rather be gathering grain in the hot sun!* After a summer of gleaning, she knew what to expect when she went to the fields every day. Boaz had been gracious toward her. However, Ruth knew that the need for food extended beyond the harvest. Threshing meant the end of gleaning. I believe that inside she felt a deep sense of hope, the same hope she must have felt on the way to Bethlehem with Naomi. With every step toward her new challenge, she must have been assured that she was doing the right thing. It had to be right to leave Moab and right to follow Naomi. It was right to have faith in Naomi's God. "Yes," I bet she whispered to herself, "there is something right about what I am about to do. Your land, your people, your God. Everything is going to be okay."

The glint of a new day brought the gift of joy and peace to the threshing floor. For Boaz, it was a day of gratitude for the expressed willingness of Ruth to be his wife. With her words, "I am your servant Ruth . . .

spread the corner of your garment over me, since you are my Kinsman-Redeemer" (Ruth 3:9), she bestowed on him great kindness and honor. His response revealed his heart of gratitude: "The Lord bless you my daughter . . . This kindness is greater than that which you showed earlier. You have not run after the younger men, whether rich or poor. And now my daughter, don't be afraid. I will do for you all you ask. All my people of my town know that you are a woman of noble character" (Ruth 3:10-11). It was a new day in the life of Boaz. His God, Yahweh, had honored him with the devotion of a woman known for her kindness and character.

For Ruth, the new day was an answer to Naomi's prayer for her: "May the Lord show kindness to you. May the Lord grant that . . . you will find rest in the home of another husband" (Ruth 1:8-9). Suddenly, the sting of widowhood was gone. Her God, Yahweh, had given her the desire of her heart—a Kinsman-Redeemer.

In the new day, Boaz would confer with the Kinsman-Redeemer who was nearer in relation than he to Naomi. It was his privilege to first redeem Naomi's land and daughter-in-law. If he declined, Boaz would buy the land and take Ruth as his wife. In the new day, Ruth would return to her mother-in-law and share with her all that had happened on the threshing floor. Before sending her off, Boaz gave Ruth a guarantee of his intentions. "'Bring me the shawl you are wearing and hold it out.' When she did so, he poured into it six measures of barley and placed the bundle on her . . . 'Don't go back to your mother-in-law empty-handed'" (Ruth 3:15-17). In this single act of generosity, Boaz said to Ruth, "What is mine is yours." Her greatest needs had been met.

You can almost hear the words of Ruth's soul. "Everything is going to be okay. Everything is going to be okay! Wait until Naomi hears this!" And hear it she did. Everything!

Boaz proceeded to act on his promise to Ruth. He called the elders of the town as witnesses and approached the Kinsman-Redeemer who could deter his hopes of marrying Ruth. After hearing the facts, the nearer kinsman yielded his privilege to Boaz. In the presence of the elders, the two legalized the transaction according to Jewish law. "One man took off his sandal and gave it to the other, and this was a confirmation in Israel." (Ruth 4:7). Sandals exchanged. Marriage on!

So Boaz took Ruth and she became his wife.
When he made love to her, the Lord enabled her to conceive,
and she gave birth to a son. The women said to Naomi:
"Praise be to the Lord, who this day has not left you without a
guardian-redeemer. May he become famous throughout Israel!
He will renew your life and sustain you in your old age.
For your daughter-in-law, who loves you and who is better
to you than seven sons, has given him birth."
Then Naomi took the child in her arms and cared for him.
The women living there said, "Naomi has a son!" And they named
him Obed. He was the father of Jesse, the father of David.
RUTH 4:13-17

Ruth's "where you go" faith was not in vain. The longer she witnessed the faithfulness of the God of Judah, the more she realized the truth about the gods of Moab. They were nothing more than sculpted stone, carved wood, and poured metal. Each of them was a lifeless idol with no power, no compassion, no provision, no protection, and no ability to forgive or bless. Oh, how Ruth must have wished that Orpah had come with them.

Ruth's fork-in-the-road decision opened her to the fullness of God's grace. She learned two principles of faith in God: "Nothing is impossible with God" (Luke 1:37) and nothing is worthwhile without God. Naomi's empty life was filled to overflowing. Boaz became a picture of the Kinsman-Redeemer of our souls—Jesus Christ. Boaz and Ruth are listed in the genealogy of the Messiah. Truly, this was a marriage made in heaven. "Okay" went beyond the wildest dreams of Ruth the Moabitess!

The Nourishment

A wife of noble character who can find?
She is worth far more than rubies.
PROVERBS 31:10

He has showed you, O man, what is good.
And what does the Lord require of you? To act justly and
to have mercy and to walk humbly with your God.
MICAH 6:8

We have arrived at the Faith Code of Conduct for our sons and daughters. Embroider the words *noble character, justice, mercy,* and *a humble walk with God* on their Growing Robes with twenty-four–karat gold thread. These words embody the nutrition of all former Faith Feedings. Proverbs 31:10 and Micah 6:8 are solid food. They are ancient words from an Almighty God that merit our full attention. Without these principles, character and integrity are absent in our men and women. Without them, how can our children succeed? How can our families survive? How can our nation be sustained? With them, godliness will prevail.

Proverbs 31:10 and Micah 6:8 speak of the character and integrity of our offspring whether male or female. When God made them "in his image . . . male and female" (Gen. 1:27), his original intent was that his human creations would bear his holy character. Nothing has changed about God's intent. While we will look at them separately for the purpose of instruction, the content of these verses is ageless, timeless, genderless, and eternal. If you have daughters, apply them both. If you have sons, do the same.

A wife of noble character who can find?
She is worth far more than rubies.
PROVERBS 31:10

If you have a daughter, pray that she grows into such a wife. If you have a son, pray that he finds such a wife. Not all of our daughters will be wives, but all wives are daughters. The focus of this verse is not marriage but rather noble character. Therefore, we should impress on our young girls the significance of character in their lives. The writer of Proverbs 31 goes on to describe the benefit for the family that noble character will produce. A wife of noble character brings benefit to her husband and children. She is industrious and generous to the poor. She brings respect to her husband and dignity to her home. Most importantly, "She speaks with wisdom, and faithful instruction is on her tongue" (Prov. 31:26). It is imperative that we as mothers model noble character and foster it in our daughters. Godly character traits are truly more precious than rubies to a future husband or wife and to society at large. Let's examine three ruby red character traits: honesty, trustworthiness, and moral fiber.

HONESTY

Honesty is difficult to teach because honesty is hard to model. The greatest lie about dishonesty is that it exists in small portions. There is no such thing as a "little lie." When the phone rings and we instruct, "Tell them I'm not here," we are modeling untruthfulness. Telling the truth can be difficult and inconvenient, but it is never lost on children. We must display an unbending standard of truth in order to cement a truth foundation in our child's character.

Let me give you the honest truth about honesty. Proverbs 12:22: "The LORD detests lying lips, but he delights in those who tell the truth" (NLT). It is your responsibility as a faith mother to instruct your children about God's view of a lying tongue. Sometimes telling the truth takes a great deal of courage. Be diligent in commending them for their courage when they choose honesty. Sometimes it takes courage for you to hold them accountable to the truth. Always, it takes your own truthfulness as an example.

TRUSTWORTHINESS

How often have you heard a child say to a parent, "You don't trust me"? Shift the focus, Mom, from your tendency not to trust, to their responsibility to earn your trust. Greater trustworthiness earns greater trust. This is played out in two ways. When your child shows that he or she is trustworthy, commend them for it. When they have earned your trust in one area, trust them with something greater. This will take you and your child from trust to trust. Move slowly in this trust building and know that the need for rebuilding trust will occur along the way. Concerning a wife of noble character, trust is the heart of a marriage relationship. I pray for your success in building credibility in your child. May you never hear the words, "You don't trust me." If you do, you might respond, "You've got that right!"

MORAL FIBER

This is a tough one in this day of moral depletion. The truth is that it is a tough one in any age. Today, however, our children face challenges to their morality in every realm of their lives. Immorality is glamorized, accepted, unedited, and often rewarded. The screens before our children, namely the television, movie, computer, and phone, scream for them to forsake their minds and bodies. The images shape their morals and dull their conscience.

When I was a young girl, I heard a sermon on 1 Corinthians 3:16: "Don't you know that you are God's temple and that God's Spirit lives in you?" (NCV). By God's grace, that Bible verse pierced my conscience. On countless occasions it played on the screen of my mind. You and I both know firsthand the temptations of our young women. Use your parental control button liberally. Monitor their peer relationships. Educate your teens to the consequences of the social media. Do not allow sitcoms, commercials, movies, or a wayward friend to set the moral standards of your home. If we do not give our girls and boys an alternative moral screen, who will? Override the message of the world with the Word of God. Overshadow their natural naivety with the guidance to make wise decisions that will bring God's blessing to their lives. Give them understanding of the consequences of their choices. Pray specifically for the moral conscience and strength of your daughters (and sons). Ask God to shield their ears and eyes from anything that would deter noble character. And do not forget to pray for their friends. Encourage your child to set the standard of noble character in his or her circle of influence.

There you have just three ruby reds of a wife of moral character: honesty, trustworthiness, and moral fiber. Keep in mind that when you repeatedly underscore God's perspective on noble character, you tighten the boundaries of the conscience of your child. Give your future son-in-law or daughter-in-law a prenuptial gift—your unwavering devotion to God's intent for godliness in the next generation. And leave the results to the One who is faithful in all generations.

> *Charm is deceptive, and beauty is fleeting; but a woman*
> *who fears the Lord is to be praised.*
> PROVERBS 31:30

"Ruby Red" is a song from this mother's heart that conveys the value of noble character in the brides of our family. I pray that you will be blessed by it as you build ruby-red character traits into those who call you Mother.

RUBY RED
(PROVERBS 31:10)

In my mind, I have seen you all of my days.
Kindness and wisdom and most noble ways have painted a picture
both precious and rare. Hearts brought together creating a pair
that spins the years with love and joy.

In my mind, I have seen you since I was a boy.
In my heart, I have known you since I was a child.
In my soul, you are held as one undefiled.
In my being, you have always stood by my side
and given me strength that cannot be denied.
With laughter and fun we chased away sad.
In my heart, I have known you since I was a lad.
In my hand, I have held yours forever it seems—
walking with you in all of my dreams.
Next to me always we face life with cheer.
Arm in arm together we have nothing to fear;
For God is our Pilot. We stand in his Truth.
In my hand, I have held yours since I was a youth.

REFRAIN

More precious than rubies this wife that I find
Standing beside me as in my mind.
Full measure to treasure all of my life.
My beauty, my bride, my friend, my wife.
My beauty, my bride, my friend, my wife.

2002 DEEDEE CASS

He has showed you, O man, what is good.
And what does the Lord require of you?
To act justly and to have mercy and
to walk humbly with your God.

MICAH 6:8

Good is a relative term. What is good to one may not be good to another. Micah 6:8 reveals what is good to God. Micah was a prophet that lived in the age of the kings of Israel. Prophets were chosen by God to deliver the message of God to his people. Micah's name means "who is like Jehovah." Micah 6:8 illuminates three character traits that God sees as good: justice, mercy, and humility. Instilling them in our sons (and daughters) will make them Micahs in their own generation—young men and women who reflect the nature of God.

My husband calls this verse our job description from God. Micah 6:8 is not a suggestion. It is a requirement. It is how we are to live as children of the living God. God desires his people to act justly, love mercy, and to walk humbly with their God. While they are in our home, our children are apprentices. Never forget the mother of influence that you are. If they emulate you, will they be on track in fulfilling God's requirement for what is good?

Zechariah, a prophet of God who lived about 250 years after Micah, said it this way: "This is what the Lord Almighty said, 'Administer true justice; show mercy and compassion to one another. Do not oppress the widow or the fatherless, the alien or the poor. Do not plot evil against each other . . . These are the things you are to do: Speak the truth to each other, and render sound judgment in your courts; do not plot evil against each other, and do not love to swear falsely. I hate all this,' declares the Lord" (Zech. 7:9-10; 8:16-17). God is the Author of justice for all, the Champion of mercy for the less fortunate, and the Essence of humility. As our heavenly Father, He desires us to emulate Him. We are apprentices of a just, merciful, and humble God.

The key to Micah 6:8 is the third requirement of walking humbly with our God. The good that God requires springs from our humble walk with Him. What is good is what is God. A walk with God is a walk of humility that deepens as we more clearly understand our own insufficiency in light of God's greatness. Do you remember Elizabeth's son, John the Baptist? After Jesus began his public ministry, John said, "He must become greater; I must become less" (John 3:30). Such is the path to a humble walk with God: more of God and less of us. Teaching humility to your apprentices is essential and challenging. In a world that relies heavily on self-enterprise and effort, humility is often viewed as weakness. Nothing could be further from the truth. The strongest place to be is in a place of reliance on the God of the universe. Humility is required for such reliance. It is humility that leads us to a need for a Savior. It is humility that lifts us up in the Savior's eyes. It is humility that is required to walk with God.

Justice, mercy, and humility originate with God and culminate in God. A life of faith produces these Godlike qualities. A child of faith grows into them. The God of faith calls them good. "He has showed you, O man, what is good. And what does the Lord require of you? To act justly and to have mercy and to walk humbly with your God" (Mic. 6:8).

> *Listen, my son, to your father's instruction and*
> *do not forsake your mother's teaching.*
> *They are a garland to grace your head and*
> *a chain to adorn your neck.*
> PROVERBS 1:8-9

Proverbs 31:10 and Micah 6:8 ask two questions that elucidate what is important to God: Where is a wife of noble character to be found and what does the Lord require of us? They relate the rarity of character and integrity and the significance of knowing God's requirements for living a faith life. Evidence of what is important to God is what we hope for in our adult children.

WHEN YOUR CHILD SAYS THAT HE OR SHE LIKES
(OR DISLIKES) ANOTHER PERSON,
ASK THEM TO TELL YOU WHY. OVER TIME,
THIS EXERCISE WILL HELP THEM RECOGNIZE AND
VALUE GODLY QUALITIES IN THEIR PEERS.

Emphasizing the value of godly character and integrity in your home will benefit your sons and daughters in two ways. It will produce noble character in their own lives and help them identify character and integrity in others. When your child says that he or she likes (or dislikes) another person, ask them to tell you why. Over time, this exercise will help them recognize and value godly qualities in their peers. It will help them be wise in their choice of friends. Eventually, one of those friends may become their spouse. You will be glad to see them use the discernment they learned at home in their relationships.

I recall what was termed the largest oil spill in American history. Is there one among us who is not affected by the pictures of those ducks helplessly floating on their backs because of the oil on their wings? The underwater images of the escape of oil from beneath the earth were awesome. In the same way, we are experiencing an integrity spill. Godly character is gushing from the faith foundation of our nation. The core of the family, government, and marketplace are threatened. To this I say, rise up, people of faith. Cap the loss of noble character. Seek God with all your heart. Speak God into your family. Act justly, love mercy, and walk humbly with your God lest that which we hold dear be as a hopeless water fowl destined for demise.

These last two Faith Feeding principles are far reaching for those with young children. Be certain, however, that the time will come when you, as a mother, will be glad you offered your child a home and your family an environment of faith principles. When they enter adulthood, you will know that God in his infinite wisdom used your children with all of their gifts and graces to build faith in the one who gave them life on this earth. Praise God for you, dear mother.

The secret things belong to the Lord our God,
but the things revealed belong to us and to our children forever,
that we may follow all the words of this law.
DEUTERONOMY 29:29

THE LESSON

There are sixty-six books in the Bible. Two of them bear the names of women—Esther and Ruth. Both of these women were used mightily in the kingdom of God. Esther, as you know, was used to save a whole nation. She was a wife of noble character to a powerful but godless king. Through Ruth, God rose up King David, who was the greatest king in the history of the Jewish nation—the very people that Esther saved from annihilation. The lives of these two women are intertwined in history. Both of them demonstrated unswerving commitment to God to the persons of influence in their lives. For Esther it was Mordecai, the cousin who became her parent. For Ruth, it was Naomi, the mother-in-law who became her mother. God used Mordecai and Naomi to accomplish his will through two ruby-red women. Do you see the priority that God places on relationships? Relationships are the faith bridges of life. They span time, culture, and society to restore the hearts of men and women to God, their Creator. The book of Ruth is the Golden Gate Bridge of Bible relationships. It bridges a gentile woman with the God of Israel. It bridges an earthly king with the King of heaven. Come then, let us walk together across this Bible bridge.

NAOMI

Naomi belies the centuries-old reputation of a mother-in law. She brings the ideal to the most ridiculed family relationship we know. Even Orpah, who chose to return to her own parents and gods, was tearful in their parting. In-laws are sometimes tagged as sources of trial and trouble in the realm of married couples. Honestly, I confess there must be some truth in this oft-spoken complaint. Naomi breaks the mold. Naomi knew the risk of taking her Hebrew sons to live in a gentile nation. It may have been one of the things she thought about on the dusty road to Moab. They would grow into manhood in Moab. It was likely that they would take wives from the Moabites. And they did, both of them. Ruth and Orpah's expressed love for the mother of their husbands tells me that Naomi looked beyond their nationality and their background. She accepted the gentile wives of her Hebrew sons and built a relationship with them. No doubt the mutual grief that these three widows shared served to cultivate their feelings toward one another.

I envision Naomi as one who displayed godly wisdom in her life. James 3:17 in the King James Version defines the wisdom of God. "But the wisdom that is from above is first pure, then peaceable, gentle and easy to be entreated, full of mercy and good fruits, without partiality, and without hypocrisy." I marked this verse in one of the Bibles I used when I first began to study the Scriptures. It is dated November of 1983. I recall the stop sign where I was when I heard on the car radio an explanation about the phrase "easy to be entreated." The radio voice said that someone who was easy to be entreated was approachable. At that moment, I understood that wisdom from above required me to be yielded to others for the purpose of sharing the God of my faith. Right then behind the wheel, I asked the Lord to make me easily approachable. I have seen the benefit of allowing the preferences of others to take priority in personal relationships. I believe that Naomi was found to be easy to be entreated by her daughters-in-law. In that way they became "daughters-in-love."

Ruth's "where you go I will go" promise to Naomi was entreated by Naomi's acceptance of Ruth as a person of value. Being fully embraced by Naomi, Ruth fully embraced Naomi and her people and her God. And Naomi built a trust relationship with Ruth, the Moabitess.

My own mother-in-law experience could be likened to the relationship between Ruth and Naomi. From the day I met Mary, she accepted all of me as if I were her own. It was enough for her that I loved her son. She expected nothing more. In God's grace, my mother was a Naomi to my husband as well. We are each eternally grateful to have had two mothers who loved us as their own. Our marriage vows have been easier kept because of those like Naomi in our lives.

I am grateful for the lessons I learned at the hand of Mary. She cherished my love of her son; she loved me as a daughter, and she trusted my way. Mame, as my father-in-law called her, was a living example of one who enabled her son to carry out the mandate of Genesis 2:24: "For this reason a man will leave his father and mother and be united to his wife, and they will become one flesh." I think that such a perspective is commendable for a mother of sons. Now, it is my turn to be a Naomi. My children-in-law have blessed my life because by faith I know they are both answers to my and my husband's prayers for our daughter and son. My personal Naomi goal is to do what they need, honor what they do, and build who they are. Such a lofty goal cannot be reached in my own strength. The words of Jesus come to mind: "My grace is sufficient for you, for my power is made perfect in weakness'" (2 Cor. 12:9). Amen to that!

At Mary's service, my husband related Micah 6:8 to the MomMom of our children. Surely, it is true. She acted justly, loved mercy, and walked humbly with her God. My sentiments were expressed with the following poem:

MARY'S GIFT

The mother of my husband has deeply graced my life,
I became her daughter when I became his wife.
She loved me as I was born of her very self;
I drank her cup of compassion and sampled all her wealth.
Before her I was flawless, no blemish did she see,
I was her cherished treasure, she loved me for me.
She thought my children perfect, and yet, in wisdom knew,
I needed understanding as through each stage they grew.
She loved the trees and flowers and cardinals and the shore.
When I gave her little, she always thought it more.
Laughter was her mainstay, simple pleasure brought her joy,
But her greatest gift to me was her little boy,
who grew to be a man that deeply loves the Lord.
That brings to his home and family the Truth that she adored,

the Truth of knowing the Shepherd and His Master Plan,
the Truth of knowing we're abiding in His steady hand.
So thank you my sweet Jesus for the Mary I have known
And the peace of knowing that she is safely home.
1993 DEEDEE CASS

Naomi was an eternal bridge builder. Across her bridge walked God's servant, Ruth. At the end of the day, God supremely blessed Naomi for her cooperation with his plan. He bestowed on her "the oil of joy instead of mourning, and a garment of praise instead of a spirit of despair" (Isa. 61:3). Can't you just see Naomi cradling her grandson, Obed, in her arms and hear her singing a soft melody of praise and thanksgiving?

RUTH

If we look at Ruth through the eyes of Boaz, we see a woman of respect and character. In the field, Ruth was known as "the Moabite who came back from Moab with Naomi" (Ruth 2:6). The news had gotten to Boaz. His appreciation for Ruth's actions toward Naomi was evident.

"I've been told all about what you have done for your mother-in-law since the death of your husband—how you left your father and mother and your homeland and came to live with a people you did not know before" (Ruth 2:11). Ruth's unselfish actions were not lost on Boaz. His words render the highest respect for the foreign woman who had come to glean in his field. Respect is built on right responses to life's situations. It must be earned, and it must be protected. As your children grow through their school years, they will have many opportunities to make decisions that will bring them the respect of others. Familiarize your young people with the concept of respect. When they demonstrate courage to act wisely or the willingness to give something up for the sake of others, say to them, "I respect you for what you have done." Your respect is the most important respect in the world to your child. Ascribe to them respect, and they will seek to be respectful. It was in respect that Ruth found favor in her efforts to glean wheat for food. Respect also brought to her Boaz's full cooperation and kindness.

When the harvest was over and the threshing began, Ruth's respect brought her abundant blessing through God's servant, Boaz. He respected her proposal that he be her Kinsman-Redeemer. Boaz's respect of Ruth overshadowed her race, her background, and her standing. As a respected man himself, he honored Ruth for her reputation. "All the people of my town know that you are a woman of noble character" (Ruth 3:11). His fellow townsmen had witnessed her kindness and compassion toward Naomi. She was industrious and humble, confident and full of charity. Ruth was a Proverbs 31 woman before her time. For Boaz, she was a keeper.

BOAZ

The Bible says that Boaz was a man of standing (Ruth 2:1). The story supports that characterization with his relationship with his workers (Ruth 2:4) and with the elders at the city gate (Ruth 4:1-12). The aspect of Boaz that touches my heart is his kindness. Naomi gives us insight on the kindness of her husband's relative from the tribe of Elimelech. When Ruth came back from the fields and shared with Naomi that she had found favor in the field of Boaz, Naomi exclaimed, "The Lord bless him . . . He has not stopped showing his kindness to the living and the dead" (Ruth 2:20). The Hebrew word for kindness in this verse is *hesed*. It can be taken to mean *loving-kindness*. It is the same word that Naomi used when she urged Orpah and Ruth to return to their own villages: "'May the Lord show kindness to you, as you have shown to your dead husbands and me" (Ruth 1:8). *Hesed* portrays kindness that comes from a heart of love. Boaz exhibited the loving-kindness of God to Naomi. It was loving-kindness that prompted our heavenly Father to give his Son as a sacrifice for the sins of the world. It is loving-kindness that Jesus imparts to us as we trust him in daily faith. It is loving-kindness that dispenses unmerited favor and abundant blessing. Nurture *hesed* in your sons and daughters. Teach them to draw from the well of God's loving-kindness and extend it to others. For Boaz, *hesed* was the marker of his life. So should it be in ours.

Ruth, Naomi, and Boaz are three people brought together for the purpose of building an eternal faith bridge. Little Obed became the father of Jesse who was the father of David. In 1 Samuel 13:14, David is described as "a man after God's own heart". Is that not our coveted goal for the fruit of our womb? I earnestly pray that God will pour out his loving-kindness on you and your family so that wherever you go, you and your people will be known as builders of bridges of faith in the one true God.

Therefore, since we are surrounded by such
a great cloud of witnesses, let us throw off everything that
hinders and the sin that so easily entangles, and let us run with
perseverance the race marked out for us. Let us fix our eyes
on Jesus, the author and perfecter of our faith.
HEBREWS 12:1-2A

THE POINT TO FAITH

A wife of noble character who can find?
She is worth far more than rubies.
PROVERBS 31:10

The standard is set. The mandate is clear and challenging. Your character matters and so does the character of your daughter and your son. Make it your personal priority to be more precious than rubies. Your model will hearten your daughter to be the same in her generation. May your son also mirror the noble character of his beloved mother.

He has showed you, O man, what is good.
And what does the Lord require of you? To act justly and
to have mercy and to walk humbly with your God.
MICAH 6:8

This verse gives definition to the noble character that is worth more than rubies. Our society sorely needs an infusion of God's justice and mercy. It will come only from a humble walk with God by those who claim to be in Christ. Do not tarry, then. Follow God's requirements in your life and family. We will all benefit from your obedience to Micah 6:8.

PRAYER: *God in heaven, I ask You to impart to me godly character. I ask You to make integrity the signpost of those You have given me. Let mercy and justice be evident in all who enter our home and to those You bring along the paths of our lives. In Jesus' Name I pray. Amen.*

THE RETURN
TO RAMAH STORY

During his lifetime, Samuel returned often to Ramah, his birthplace. On one such occasion, he visited the family homestead. When he entered the door, he could almost feel the presence of his faithful parents, Elkanah and Hannah. He stood for a moment and looked around trying to take in the simple beauty of the place he called home. He glanced toward the loft and saw something he had never seen before. *How could I have missed the wooden box that was pushed against the back wall?* he thought. Like a child he climbed the ladder quickly. Kneeling beside the chest, he was suddenly struck with a sense of awe. The meaning of his name was crudely etched on the top—Heard of God. His mother had told him why he was named Samuel many times. It was her favorite story. His hands rubbed over the wood as he pictured Hannah's joyful face when she came to see him in Shiloh. When he opened the old wooden chest, his heart and mind were flooded with untold emotion. As if preserved for this very day, the chest contained all the linen ephod robes that he had worn to minister in the house of the Lord as a child. They were neatly folded and stacked with the smallest on top.

He remembered receiving each robe. They were always a little big at first. But, he grew into each one perfectly. Suddenly he realized that his mother somehow knew exactly how large to make her yearly gift. For the first time, he considered the sacrificial love of his mother, Hannah. She had given her firstborn son up to the Lord's service when he was a toddler. As an old man, he knew that her sacrifice was not in vain. God had used him mightily in the course of his lifetime. He remembered how the Lord called his name in the night. He had thought it was Eli calling. But Eli said it wasn't him. The third time he'd gone to the priest, Eli told him it was the Lord calling him. Eli had instructed him," Go and lie down and if he calls you say, 'Speak, Lord, for your servant is listening.'" He had done as Eli instructed and "The Lord came and stood there, calling as at the other times, 'Samuel! Samuel!'" (1 Sam. 3:8-10). From that time on, the Lord had blessed Samuel with the special gift of hearing and speaking the Word of God.

Two highlights of his life played in his mind. He had the privilege of anointing Saul, the first king of Israel. He also recalled the time when Jesse, the son of Obed, brought his seven sons to him. God had said that one of them would be the next king of Israel. From the oldest to the youngest they passed before him. He thought each one to be the right one, but God said He had not chosen any of them. Samuel could still hear the exchange between himself and Jesse.

"Are these all the sons you have?"

"There is still the youngest but he is tending the sheep."

"Send for him; we will not sit down until he arrives."

Eventually, the young shepherd son of Jesse came and stood before Samuel. As clearly as if God were next to him, Samuel heard the words of the Lord. "Rise and anoint him; he is the one" (1 Sam. 16:11-12). And David became king of Israel.

Tears flowed down Samuel's worn and ruddy face. For the first time, he understood that each accomplishment in his life as a prophet of the Lord and judge of Israel came in answer to his mother's prayers. No doubt she had prayed for his safety and protection as well. More than once he was in great danger from the Philistines. With hands raised to the heavens, Samuel praised God for the mother who had had the faith to believe in her son and the heart to give him up to the Lord for all the days of his life. He would never stop thanking God for the influence of his godly mother on his life of meaning and purpose.

———————

WITH HANDS RAISED TO THE HEAVENS,
SAMUEL PRAISED GOD FOR THE MOTHER WHO HAD
HAD THE FAITH TO BELIEVE IN HER SON AND
THE HEART TO GIVE HIM UP TO THE LORD
FOR ALL THE DAYS OF HIS LIFE.

———————

With hands raised to the heavens, Samuel praised God for the mother who had had the faith to believe in her son and the heart to give him up to the Lord for all the days of his life.

> *Her children arise and call her blessed;*
> *her husband also, and he praises her:*
> *Many women do noble things,*
> *but you surpass them all.*
> PROVERBS 31:28-29

> *The life of mortals is like grass,*
> *they flourish like a flower of the field;*
> *the wind blows over it and it is gone,*
> *and its place remembers it no more.*
> *But from everlasting to everlasting*
> *the Lord's love is with those who fear him,*
> *and his righteousness with their children's children—*
> *with those who keep his covenant*
> *and remember to obey his precepts.*
> PSALM 103:15-18

CONNECT WITH DEEDEE:

A companion study guide to *Faith Feedings*
is available for download,
along with other resources, at:
www.DeeDeeCass.com

Follow DeeDee's faith nurturing blog at
www.thegrowingrobe.com

Another book by DeeDee Cass:
The Scripture Code...unlocking spiritual wealth

Other Recommended Faith Resources:
communitybiblestudy.org
scriptureunion.org
CRU.org

Prayer may indeed be a parent's most important work. For over two decades, *Lord, Bless My Child* has helped edify families through the power of prayer. Inside this beautiful gift book, you'll find:

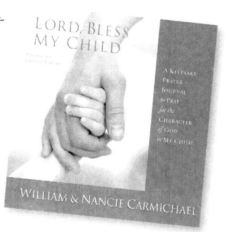

- A template to guide parents in praying for the character of God to be developed in the lives of their children.
- 52 prayer concepts that align with God's plan for each child.
- Scriptures, prayers, and age-old quotes.
- Discussion questions for family interaction.
- A place to journal your prayers—and later to add how God has answered.

Grandparents and parents will enjoy sharing this book as they teach their family to pray. Many parents present the completed journal to their child as a gift when they leave home, so they can see how God answered their parents' prayers over the years.

A meaningful gift for expectant mothers, as well as the perfect gift for pastors to present to parents during baby dedications and baptisms. Preserve your family's unique testimony of God's enduring love and faithfulness with *Lord, Bless My Child!*

Available at Amazon, Barnes and Noble, and bookstores everywhere.

CPSIA information can be obtained at www.ICGtesting.com
Printed in the USA
BVOW02s2058040615

402773BV00006B/2/P